An IEEE Guide

How to Find What You Need in the Bluetooth™ Spec

Tom Siep

Published by
Standards Information Network
IEEE Press

Trademarks and disclaimers

IEEE believes the information in this publication is accurate as of its publication date; such information is subject to change without notice. IEEE is not responsible for any inadvertent errors.

Library of Congress Cataloging-in-Publication Data

Siep, Tom, 1947-
An IEEE guide: how to find what you need in the Bluetooth Spec / authored by Tom Siep.
  p. cm.
  ISBN 0-7381-2635-7 (paperback) —ISBN 0-7381-2636-5 (pdf)
    1. Bluetooth technology (Standard) 2. Telecommunication—
Equipment and supplies. 3. Computer network protocols. I. Title.

TK5103.3 .S54 2000
004.6'2—dc21   *00-050537*

The Institute of Electrical and Electronics Engineers, Inc.
3 Park Avenue, New York, NY 10016-5997, USA

Copyright © 2001 by the Institute of Electrical and Electronics Engineers, Inc. All rights reserved. Printed in the United States of America.

No part of this publication may be reproduced in any form, in an electronic retrieval system or otherwise, without the prior written permission of the publisher.

IEEE Press/Standards Information Network (SIN) publications are not consensus documents. Information contained in this and other works has been obtained from sources believed to be reliable, and reviewed by credible members of IEEE Technical Societies, Standards Committees and/or Working Groups, and/or relevant technical organizations. Neither the IEEE not its authors guarantee the accuracy or completeness of any information published herein, and neither the IEEE nor its authors shall be responsible for any errors, omissions, or damages arising out of the use of this information.

Likewise, while the author and publisher believe that the information and guidance given in this work serve as an enhancement to users, all parties must rely upon their own skill and judgement when making use of it. Neither the author nor the publisher assumes any liability to anyone for any loss or damage caused by any error or omission in the work, whether such error or omission is the result of negligence or any other cause. Any and all such liability is disclaimed.

This work is published with the understanding that the IEEE and its authors are supplying information through this publication, not attempting to render engineering or other professional services. If such services are required, the assistance of an appropriate professional should be sought. The IEEE is not responsible for the statements and opinions advanced in the publication.

Review Policy

The information contained in IEEE Press/Standards Information Network publications is reviewed and evaluated by peer reviewers of relevant IEEE Technical Societies, Standards Committees and/or Working Groups, and/or relevant technical organizations. The authors addressed all of the reviewers' comments to the satisfaction of both the IEEE Standards Information Network and those who served as peer reviewers for this document.

The quality of the presentation of information contained in this publication reflects not only the obvious efforts of the authors, but also the work of these peer reviewers. The IEEE Press acknowledges with appreciation their dedication and contribution of time and effort on behalf of the IEEE.

To order IEEE Press Publications, call 1-800-678-IEEE.

Print: ISBN 0-7381-2635-7 SP1121
PDF: ISBN 0-7381-2636-5 SS1121

See other standards and standards-related product listings at:
http://standards.ieee.org/

Acknowledgment

This *Guide* began with the tireless efforts of Ian Gifford to further the cause of creating a book that makes the Bluetooth™ wireless communications technology accessible to a wide range of readers. During the past two years as Chair of IEEE 802.15.1 and IEEE liaison to the Bluetooth Special Interest Group, his efforts have been invaluable. To me, Ian has been a cheerleader, mentor, driver, and friend. This *Guide* would not have happened without him.

My friend and colleague, Carl Panasik, provided vital material and insight for the discussions on the radio frequency aspects of the Bluetooth wireless technology.

I would also like to thank the reviewers who took the time and effort to read and comment on early drafts of this work. Their efforts are greatly appreciated and resulted in a much better book. The Reviewers' names and affiliations are listed below.

> Tom Baker, Lucent Technologies
> Chatschik Bisdikian, IBM Corporation
> Ian Gifford, M/A-COM, and AMP Division
> Jon Inouye, Intel Corporation
> Susan McNeil, Lucent Technologies
> Lou Wallace, Baylor Senior Healthcare System
> Also, there was one anonymous reviewer.

The IEEE editorial staff in the persons of Susan Tatiner, Jennifer Longman, and Yvette Ho Sang has exhibited patience, wisdom, kindness, and fortitude in guiding me through the process of creating this Guide.

Finally, I want to thank my own personal proofreader, stenographer, editor, counselor, friend, soul mate, and wife, Anne.

-Tom Siep

About the Author

Tom Siep is a Group Member of the Technical Staff in the Wireless Communications Business Unit of Texas Instruments (TI). He is responsible for coordinating Short Distance Wireless communications Research and Development.

Mr. Siep has twenty-five years of experience in many facets of communications and information systems, ranging from mainframes to embedded systems to Human Factors research. In the last fifteen years, he has championed the cause of Local Area and Personal Area Wireless communications at TI by providing technical leadership in the implementation of several pilot wireless communications systems for TI customers.

He has been a long time participant in the IEEE Standards process in both IEEE 802.11 and 802.15. Currently, he is the Chief Technical Editor for the IEEE 802.15.1 standardization of portions of the Bluetooth™ Specification.

Mr. Siep has a Bachelors degree in Management from the University of California at Fullerton and a Masters degree in Information Systems from the University of Texas at Dallas.

The digital camera is transmitting a digital postcard via a cell phone using Bluetooth wireless technology

Foreword

In 1952, digital data communications did not exist, and the total estimated number of needed computers was seven. When the ability to move information between computers was invented, their utility increased. This also drove their deployment and development.

The easy exchange of information between computers revolutionized their perceived value. These devices became part of the paper-based information systems of businesses. As computers became more capable, they gradually assumed more and more responsibilities.

The original paper-to-electron-to-paper systems have long since given way to more and more, smaller and smaller, interconnected computers. Instead of one computer for a million people, we now have tens of computers (or information handling tools) per person. As these tens of computers soon become hundreds, wires no longer remain an acceptable way to interconnect.

Wireless interconnection of personal electronic data tools is what Bluetooth™ Wireless Technology is all about.

Contents

Chapter 1	Introduction	1
	How to Use This Guide	2
	Guide to Reading the Bluetooth Specification	4
	Readers	6
	Conventions Used in the Specification	6
	Bluetooth Document Structure	9
	Layers versus Blocks	9
	Profiles are the Key to Interoperation	10
	Message Sequence Charts	10
Chapter 2	Technology Summary	17
	A Wireless World	19
	Building a Wireless Information Tool	22
	Radio	22
	Low Power	23
	Intelligence	23
	Bluetooth Environments	23
	Airplanes	25
	Distances to Expect	26
	Social Changes	27
Chapter 3	Bluetooth Applications	31
	Simple User Applications	31
	A Complex Application	33
Chapter 4	Section-By-Section Summary	37
	Radio	38
	Scope	39
	Frequency Band and Channel Arrangement	40
	Transmitter Characteristics	41

Receiver Characteristics 41
Testing Parameters 42
Baseband 43
  General Description 45
  Physical Channel 48
  Physical Link 48
  Packet Formats 49
  Error Correction 51
  Logical Channels 52
  Data Whitening 53
  Transmit/Receive Routines 54
  Transmit/Receive Timing 54
  Channel Control 55
  Hop Selection 56
  Audio Interface 58
  Device Addressing 59
  Security 60
LMP 62
  General Overview 63
  Format of LMP Messages 63
  Procedure Rules and Protocol Data
    Unit Definitions 64
  Connection Establishment 69
  A Summary of PDUs 69
  Test Modes 69
  Error Handling 70
L2CAP 70
  Introduction 71
  General Operation 73
  State Machine 74
  Data Packet Format 74
  Signaling 75
  Configuration Parameter Options 76
  Service Primitives 76

- Configuration Message Sequence Charts 76
- Implementation Guidelines 77
- SDP 77
  - Introduction 78
  - Overview 78
  - Data Representation 79
  - Protocol Description 79
  - Service Attribute Definitions 79
  - Background Information 81
  - Example SDP Transactions 81
- Communication Interfaces 82
  - RFCOMM with TS 07.10 82
  - IrDA Interoperability 84
  - Telephony Control Specification 87
  - Interoperability Requirements for Bluetooth as a WAP Bearer 88
- HCI 89
  - Bluetooth Host Controller Interface Functional Specification 90
  - HCI USB Transport Layer 92
  - HCI RS232 Transport Layer 92
  - HCI UART Transport Layer 93
- Testing 94
  - Bluetooth Test Mode 94
  - Compliance Requirements 95
  - Test Control Interface 96
- Profiles 97
  - Generic Access Profile 99
  - Service Discovery Profile Application Profile 100
  - Cordless Telephony Profile 100
  - Intercom Profile 101
  - Serial Port Profile 101

An IEEE Guide: How to Find What You Need in the Bluetooth Spec

	Headset Profile 102
	Dial-up Networking Profile 102
	Fax Profile 103
	LAN Access Profile 103
	Generic Object Exchange Profile 104
	Object Push Profile 104
	File Transfer Profile 105
	Synchronization Profile 106
	Appendices 107
Chapter 5	Consolidated Glossary 111
Chapter 6	Bluetooth Special Interest Group 135
	Bluetooth Documents 137
	Further Resources 137

Trademarks

Bluetooth is a trademark owned by Telefonaktiebolaget L M Ericsson, Sweden, and licensed to promoters and adopters of the Bluetooth Special Interest Group.

Ericsson is the trademark or registered trademark of Telefonaktiebolaget L M Ericsson, Sweden.

IBM is a registered trademark of International Business Machines Corporation in the United States, other countries, or both.

Intel is a registered trademark of Intel Corporation.

IrDA is a registered trademark of the Infrared Data Association.

Lucent and Lucent Technologies are registered trademarks of Lucent Technologies Incorporated.

Microsoft is a trademark of Microsoft Corporation in the United States and/or other countries.

Motorola is a registered trademark of Motorola Incorporated.

Nokia is a registered trademark of Nokia Corporation.

3Com is a registered trademark of 3Com Corporation.

Toshiba is a registered trademark of Toshiba Corporation.

Introduction

This IEEE Guide provides a technical overview of the Bluetooth communications system.

The Bluetooth™ system is officially defined in an

> ### Chapter 1
> · How to Use this Guide
> · Guide to Reading the Spec
> · Readers
> · Conventions used in the Spec
> · Bluetooth Document Structure
> · Layers versus Blocks
> · Profiles
> · Message Sequence Charts

imposing technical specification published by the Bluetooth Special Interest Group. This Guide will make the technology easier to understand by providing introductory, background, and summary information, as well as references.

This first chapter sets the stage for understanding both this book and the Bluetooth Specification. The basic formats of the Spec, as well as target audiences and information that might concern them, are covered here.

Once the introductions are out of the way, the "real" information begins in the *Technology Summary* in Chapter 2.

Examples of how Bluetooth wireless technology is currently being used (and will be used) are included in Chapter 3, *Bluetooth Applications*. Of course, Bluetooth applications are the reason the technology exists!

Chapter 1: Introduction

The Bluetooth Specification itself is meant to be read by those who will be creating or integrating this technology, but it can be difficult for the first-time reader to find the right area to read. The *Section-by Section Summary* in Chapter 4 furnishes quick references to where information can be found in the Spec.

The *Consolidated Acronym and Glossary* listing in Chapter 5 makes the process of deciphering the obscure words and abbreviations within the Spec easier. While the Bluetooth Spec does contain these definitions, they are spread throughout the document set in inconsistent places and formats. This *Glossary* puts them all in one place in a consistent manner.

Chapter 6 contains an annotated listing of further resources for understanding aspects of the Spec.

How to Use This Guide

Communications technology is a complex subject. This IEEE Guide is designed to streamline the process of finding (or re-finding) information about Bluetooth wireless technology. Many people will find that they use this Guide in several different ways over time.

The first use of this Guide often will be to get an overview of the technology and to determine what it is and how it can be useful. A linear reading of this Guide with occasional references to the Specification itself (more about this in **Conventions Used in the Specification** on page 6) will satisfy this need.

Once the decision has been made to study the text of the Specification more closely, the IEEE Guide will serve as a ready reference for finding information on a topic of particular interest. This is where the graphical map shown in Figure 1 and the *Section-by-Section Summary* chapter come in handy.

Codename: Bluetooth

It may seem a bit strange to name a method of communication after what seems to be a dental problem. Of course, it is not. It was named after a person in history, who likely did not have such a problem.

The technology described in the Bluetooth Specification for a small form factor, low-cost, wireless communications system was originally developed in parallel by several of the promoter companies. These originators realized that to be truly useful, many companies must become involved in the final definition. Thus, the Bluetooth Special Interest Group (Bluetooth SIG) was formed.

Current corporate customs dictate that when a project is begun, it must have a name that is at best obscurely connected to the end product. Since two of the originating companies are Scandinavian based, the name of an ancient Viking king was used. (See Who was Bluetooth? on page 9.) As sometimes happens, the code name stuck, and the technology is still called Bluetooth wireless technology.

When an area of concentration is selected, the *Consolidated Acronym and Glossary* listing in Chapter 5 will help to make sense out of the alphabet soup. This is especially important since some sections of the Spec assume definitions cited several sections previously.

Guide to Reading the Bluetooth Specification

The Bluetooth Specification itself is a 1,500+ page document published on the web at www.bluetooth.com. Not everyone will have the need (or desire) to read it all.

The first part of the document is the *Core*. It gives a picture of the technology in traditional slices, starting at the radio as the foundation and working upward. The second part—Part K— is the *Profiles*. The Profiles take a vertical slice of the technology for each of several applications. (More about this in **Conventions used in the Specification** on page 6.) See Figure 1 for an overview of the Bluetooth Specification.

Taken as a whole, the Bluetooth Specification describes a complete picture of a communications scheme. This is often referred to as a "protocol stack" or just "protocol." Protocols describe how devices of different kinds (or from different manufacturers) can get along. Communications protocols specify a set of rules that are agreed upon for the interchange of information. These rules ideally cover every possible situation so that no communications problem arises without a ready remedy.

Chapter 1: Introduction

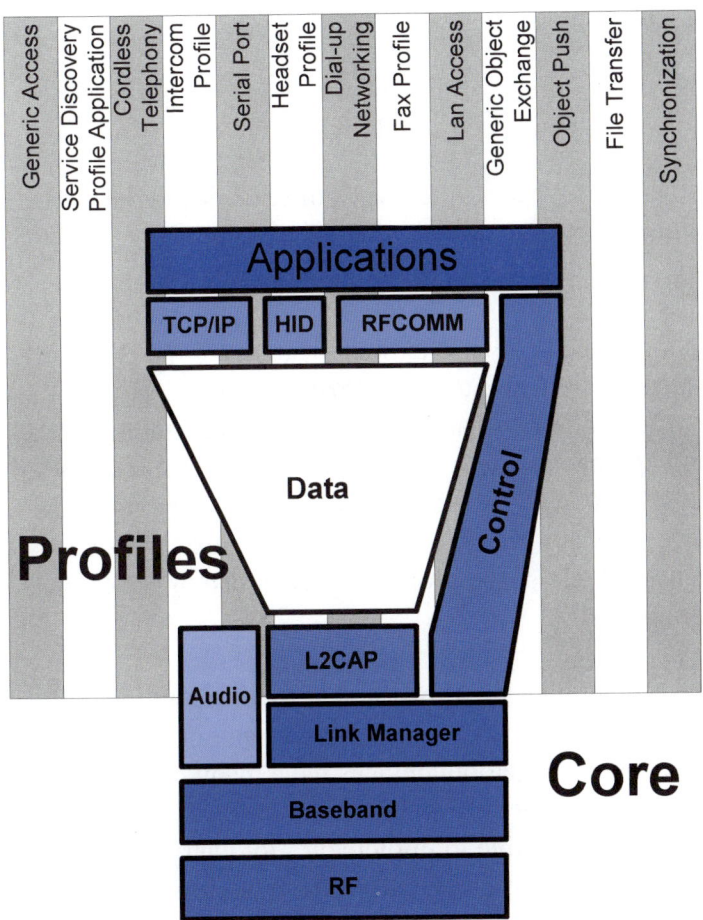

Figure 1—Overview of Bluetooth Specification

Readers

The sheer volume of the Specification prompts the question: Which audience should read what?

Table 1 describes several types of readers and the documents or sections of documents that most apply to them.

Conventions Used in the Specification

As mentioned earlier, the Specification for the Bluetooth system is divided into logical parts, the *Core* and the *Profiles*. The first part, the Core, takes the traditional layered approach to describing a protocol stack. It starts at the lowest level, the Radio, and works its way up to the more software-oriented upper layers. It describes the many features of the protocol stack, some of which are optional.

The second part, the Profiles, takes a different view of the same subject. It is a vertical rather than horizontal treatment. Since Bluetooth devices have many different levels of capability, not all features of the protocol are necessary, or are even possible to implement, for every device. This prompts the question: What needs to be implemented in each class of device to ensure that applications in devices from different manufacturers can hold meaningful interchanges? The answer lies in the Profiles. They are vertical slices of the Bluetooth protocol that call out exactly what must be implemented for a given application to

Chapter 1: Introduction

Table 1

Who	What to read
General Reader—people interested in basic concepts	Primarily this book, with introductory material from www.bluetooth.com and selected introductions to Bluetooth Specification *Core*.
Technologists—people evaluating competing technologies to select the one most appropriate for their application	Essentially the same as the General Reader with the addition of White Papers from www.bluetooth.com. The Consolidated Glossary (Chapter 5) will prove useful for establishing the vocabulary of this technology.
Systems Implementers—people with the responsibility for creating a hardware implementation of the Bluetooth wireless technology	Those who will implement Bluetooth modules will usually skip the Technology Summary (Chapter 2) and go directly into the Section-by-Section summaries in Chapter 4 for the Radio, Baseband, LPM, and L2CAP, and then into the Specification text itself. The definitions provided by the Consolidated Glossary will help to minimize the need for referring to other sections of the Specification. An understanding of the HCI will complete the required information.
System Integrators—people who take the implementations and use them to create whole systems	Engineers responsible for defining and coordinating subsystems into a functioning product will need grounding in the *Core*, then specific knowledge of *Profiles* covering that product.
Application Programmers—people who create the programs that utilize Bluetooth wireless technology	Applications writers will primarily be concerned with the *Profiles* that apply to their area. An understanding of the requirements of the HCI will aid in allowing for module interface issues for applications.

Chapter 1: Introduction

conform to Bluetooth Specifications. Additionally, the profiles provide the "glue" between the Bluetooth wireless technology and existing communications and application standards or practices.

Understanding the Core is a prerequisite to utilizing the Profiles. The order of reading the sections is important. The first section, the Radio, must be read first. Each of the following three sections build on terms and concepts presented in the previous section.

With a single exception, all the Profiles can be read independently. That single exception is the Generic Access Profile. That Profile (the first one) is a base requirement for all the other Profiles and must be satisfied, at least in part, by every Bluetooth profile.

A Bluetooth Standard?

The protocol described in the Bluetooth Specification is not really a Standard, per se. The term "Standard" has a specific meaning. It means that the material was at least reviewed and approved in an open Standards organization, such as the Institute of Electrical and Electronics Engineers, Inc. (IEEE) or the European Telecommunications Standards Institute (ETSI).

In common usage, however, there has been what is termed as an "Industry Standard" or "De facto Standard." These are specifications, such as Bluetooth, that are created in a relatively closed cooperative effort among a small group of companies.

Chapter 1: Introduction

> ### *Who was Bluetooth?*
>
> Harald Blätand was King of Denmark from 940-981, son of Gorm the Old (King of Denmark) and Thyra Danebod (daughter of King Ethelred of England). His last name translates to "Bluetooth," but it probably wasn't because of his smile. The Scandinavians are often fond of puns: his name was descriptive, but probably "Dark skinned" (blä) "Great man" (tan). Since it was a short, funny step to Blätand, he became "Bluetooth."
>
> Harald is credited with successfully merging Viking and European cultures. The Bluetooth wireless technology's namesake established a new *transcultural* mode of communication.

Bluetooth Document Structure

The structure of the Bluetooth Specification follows the common conventions of most protocol descriptions. Letters designate major sections, referred to as "parts." Sometimes subparts are further defined with a colon and a numeric qualifier. Parts "A" though "I" define the Core and the constituent subsections of Part "K" define the Profiles. There is no Part "J."

Layers versus Blocks

Traditional protocol definitions, such as those defined by IEEE or ETSI, have a fairly strict horizontal layering of functions. These layers look like stacked bricks and are almost always based on the International Standards Organization's Open Systems Interconnection (ISO OSI) Standard. Bluetooth's functions are represented in their diagrams more like a mosaic than a stack of bricks. It can be argued that this makes the Bluetooth protocol a bit more efficient, but it also makes it a bit harder for the novice to understand.

Profiles are the Key to Interoperation

The Core lays out all the possible interactions and recovery procedures. This is the pallet from which applications must draw their utility. The pallet defined by the Bluetooth wireless technology is very large.

The key concept in protocols is interoperation (often called interoperability). The concept is that if two communicating systems don't follow the same rules, they will not be able to perform the desired task.

Since applications use only a subset of the available Bluetooth pallet, a mechanism is necessary to call out the specific subset to use. The Profiles perform that function.

Message Sequence Charts

A key part to understanding the Bluetooth protocol is the set of Message Sequence Charts (MSCs) that are liberally distributed throughout both the Core and the Profiles. MSCs are protocol scenarios that illustrate a sample interaction between two communicating devices (Hosts). They also frequently illustrate interactions between constituent parts of the protocol suite residing in the Hosts.

It is important to note that MSCs do not exhaustively list all possible interactions; they only list successful, sample transactions. Error conditions, with their recovery procedures, are rarely represented in the MSCs.

The notation used in the MSCs is fairly simple. A purely fictitious example is shown in Figure 2. The MSC consists of hexagons, boxes, lines, arrows, and C-style comments set on a grid representing the end users and usually some intermediate protocol entity.

The hexagon indicates the condition that is needed to start the transaction in question. There is generally one hexagon per MSC.

Boxes have two functions. They replace a group of transactions and indicate the beginning of an alternate series of events. The former can be thought of as what programmers call a "subroutine." The latter is generally indicated by the phrase "Sub-Scenario n:". Where sub-scenarios exist, they can be considered completely independent of each other. They may be executed optionally, consequently, or exclusively.

An arrow represents a message, a signal, or a transaction. They are where the action is. The arrowhead indicates the direction of the information flow and the text associated with it describes the content. The flow is time-dependent, with time increasing from top to bottom. The subscenarios are, of course, in independent time frames.

Comments provided in the MSCs are meant to clarify what is going on during the procedure. Figure 3 is an example of the switch of responsibilities for two devices. The comments, delimited by the ancient C programming convention of slashes and asterisks, document the internal state of each participant.

Chapter 1: Introduction

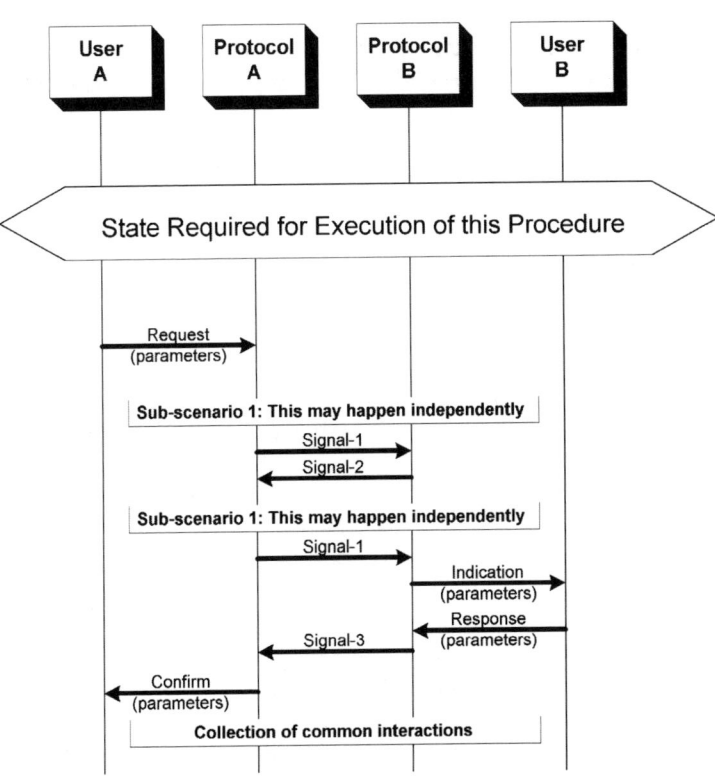

Figure 2—Example notation used in message sequence charts

Chapter 1: Introduction

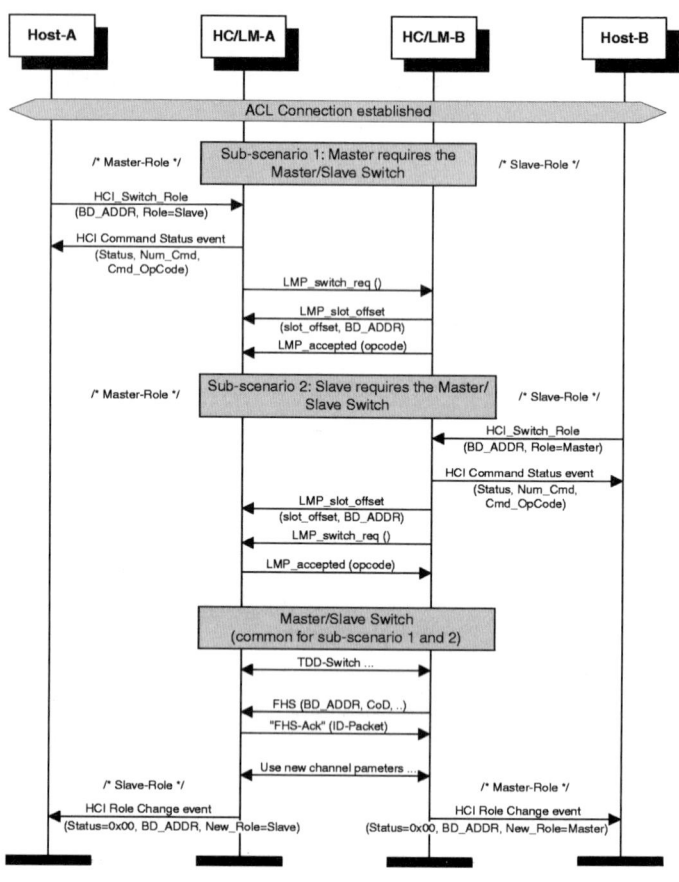

Figure 3—Example message sequence chart
Master/Slave switch: two sub-scenarios

Chapter 1: Introduction

Masters and Slaves

The Bluetooth Specification uses the politically incorrect convention for describing the relationship between the entity that controls communications and other participants. Masters decide who should communicate and when they should do it. Slaves obey their Masters. The method of organization that they adopt is called a "piconet."

An alternative description to the Master/Slave setup often used in telecommunications is Time Division Multiple Access or TDMA, where the cellular base stations manage the use of the airwaves by the terminals (cell phones).

The style of TDMA that the Bluetooth wireless technology uses is essentially a fixed TDMA. Slots are defined and allocated by the Master and left in place during the existence of the piconet. Other TDMA schemes allow for a dynamic allocation of slots and/or slot times.

As with base stations and terminals, the members of a piconet never "talk" to each other, only to the Master.

In any case, the terms Master and Slave are used only to connote that one of the entities in the piconet is in control and the others do what they are told.

Technology Summary

Consumer devices are becoming more intelligent. Part of that intelligence is their capacity to remember. Our cell phones, for exam-

> Chapter 2
> · A Wireless World
> · Building a Wireless Information Tool
> · Bluetooth Environments
> · Social Changes

ple, have the capacity to remember not only who we call frequently, but what phone calls have been tried, made, answered, or not answered.

What happens when we want this information on some other device?

Connecting wires between consumer devices is the simplest way of moving personal electronic information. Over such wires, manufacturers can, and usually do, run proprietary communication protocols. Proprietary cable links between devices have a major drawback in that the consumer usually needs to buy custom proprietary adapters for diverse devices, or else purchase all personal consumer devices from a single manufacturer. The average consumer generally won't stand for either option.

Even if the electronics world were to adopt a common wired interface standard, such as Universal Serial Bus (USB), the large number of information devices that will be operating in a person's personal operating space (POS) makes it infeasible to use wires. The increasing number of interconnections that will exist will require something other than the historic point-to-point approach.

There is a simple way of dividing information tools into two camps—things that move and things that stay put for some period of time. If everything stayed put, there are some clever methods of using alternate paths for information exchange. Phone line approaches, such as Home PNA (http://www.homepna.org/), and powerline approaches, such as HomePlug Powerline Alliance (http://www.homeplug.org/), work well for devices that do not move often.

> **Information tools**
>
> Humans have often been described as the toolmaker. As we advance in technology and increase the amount of knowledge and information that each person is exposed to and is expected to maintain, it is natural that we invent tools to help us handle this added burden. These tools are the objects that save, transmit, display, and allow us to manipulate the information that we now must cope with.

This solves the problem of interconnecting things that stay put, but it does not solve the problem of highly portable, highly personal information tools. Since the two must be able to interact, the entire problem remains unsolved.

Let's analyze the characteristics of those two kinds of personal information tools. As noted, there are two classes of information connections. One is associated more with a

Chapter 2: Technology Summary

person's physical space than any particular geographic area; the other is attached to a spot somehow and becomes connected when we come into proximity. As we move, we want to maintain contact among the items we carry with us and establish contact to local fixed objects when and if necessary. What we don't want to have to do is physically connect to devices that we pass or physically interconnect things we carry. What we need is a communications bubble that is highly portable and does not depend on physical contact.

A Textile Analogy

The increasingly complex paths of communication that are required to interconnect a large number of personal information devices is like the creation of fabric. That process is essentially:

Fiber → Thread → Weave → Fabric

The progression of information interchange is:

Point-to-Point → LAN → Internet → Ubiquitous Connectivity

A Wireless World

The alternative to wires that tie us to a particular space is to create a wireless means of transferring information. Once the decision is made on a wireless approach, one must decide what kind of wireless system makes the most

Chapter 2: Technology Summary

sense. Three approaches immediately come to mind.

- Sound
- Light
- Radio

Obviously we do not want to create an unacceptable presence with the first two options, so we will assume that the sound is beyond our (and our dog's) hearing, and the light will be light we cannot see.

Sound has been used as a wireless medium for quite awhile. In fact, a lot of the early remotes for televisions were based on an ultrasonic system. The problem with sound is that it doesn't go very far when it is at these ultra-high frequencies, and it bounces around a lot, so it really doesn't have very much data-carrying capability.

Using light as a medium for wireless communications is quite a bit more popular. That, of course, is what replaced

---

Bluetooth Devices

Just what kinds of information tools are becoming available with Bluetooth connectivity?

Cell phones   **Computers**   **Headsets**

Personal digital assistants   **Cable TV boxes**   **Data access points**

Cars   **Refrigerators**   **Watches**

...more things that store information

...things that don't store information now (but will)

Chapter 2: Technology Summary

the ultrasonic control links for television and stereo equipment. A primary example of a high-capacity, light-based system is infrared (IR). The Infrared Data Association (IrDA®) publishes specifications for developing interoperable IR solutions. IrDA, as most people who have a notebook will agree, is not necessarily the easiest system to use. In fact, although most notebooks now have IrDA ports, most of those ports have never been used. Why? The problem with light is that it must be pointed relatively precisely and most people don't particularly like that idea. Additionally, light doesn't go through walls, which is usually not a problem for using light in general, but it is a problem when communicating for more than a few feet in distance.

That leaves us with radio. Radio in the past has suffered from its own problems; it has been fairly expensive and the bandwidths and resistance to noise have been minimal. Continuing advances in radio, especially as fueled by the cellular telephone revolution, have enabled engineers to make increasingly smaller and better radios, which are also less and less expensive. This now makes radio the best choice for a wireless medium. It doesn't have the directionality or the bandwidth shortcomings that the other two mediums have.

> **What Kind of Radio is This?**
> - Frequency hopping spread spectrum
> - 2.4 GHz
> - 10-100 m range
> - ISM band for global usability

Chapter 2: Technology Summary

Building a Wireless Information Tool

Several things must happen to make this wireless world work, the most important of which is to build a workable information tool.

In order to build an information tool that is truly mobile, we'll need to add the following:

- Small radios with the appropriate attributes
- Low power portable systems
- Device intelligence

Radio

The radio is the heart of this liberating technology. In order to have freedom of movement, the information lifeline has to be well suited for its task. If it is not, the whole concept fails.

There are several attributes that a radio needs for extremely portable application. The radio must be small, light, low power, have robust communications, and be inexpensive. The radio is the facilitator for the information tool. It must not consume a great deal of the resources needed in order to make that data tool useful.

Chapter 2: Technology Summary

Low Power

The information tool itself must be low power. High power consumption means the information tool is a large size and/or it is heavy. The goal has to be that it must drive the information tools' characteristics towards its cheap competition, which in this case might be a stack of papers. Papers generally have very low power consumption.

Intelligence

The wireless medium is a relatively slow and sometimes faulty information path. Intelligence about what to transmit and when to do it can help to overcome this deficit.

As these devices become more and more intelligent, they will figure out better and better ways to minimize the use of the communication path. The more that information tools can store and analyze locally, the less communications will be necessary.

It is not that we want to prevent communications; it is just that we want to minimize the bottleneck.

Bluetooth Environments

Bluetooth wireless technology will be expected to operate in many different environments. This will range from the

Chapter 2: Technology Summary

office, in transit (in cars, buses, trains), in the home, and even perhaps in airplanes. In the office, Bluetooth personal information devices will be expected to interconnect and interact with things such as printers, the local area network, and various other information spigots that are available in the corporate infrastructure. While in transit you may need to communicate with someone you meet, or you may need to work by interconnecting a cell phone, a notebook, or other such device. Once you're at home, you'll

The Simple Radio

Radio communications design is sort of an exact science. If you get it exactly right, it works. If you don't, you may not be able to tell why it doesn't work. Unlike digital design, the analog-oriented radio designs must take into account the shades of gray of the real, messy world.

In general, the more complex the radio design, the more likely it is to be able to go farther, faster. These more complex radios have more things that could be incorrect. Also, with complexity comes some negatives such as increased cost, power consumption, volume, and weight. All these attributes need to be minimized for personal portable information tools.

The Bluetooth approach is to define a simple radio that does not depend as much on having every parameter of its design precisely honed. Its design parameters are very "loose," compared to other wireless technology such as cellular telephones.

The result is a simple, low-cost system that is straightforward enough to be able to consider integrating the entire communications function on a single chip.

have the need to interact with your home information system, which contains the repository of information that has accumulated since you were last home. You may also want to issue control commands such as turning on the lights in the house.

Airplanes

The use of Bluetooth wireless communications on airplanes presents an interesting problem. Note that the Bluetooth Specification does not say that usage in an airplane is okay, but this will likely occur anyway. Traditionally, airlines have been very skeptical, if not fearful, about any radio device that transmits while the airplane is in flight. Up to this point, it has been fairly obvious to the airline personnel when someone is using a radio device, such as a wireless mouse or a cellular phone. With Bluetooth wireless communication, however, it may not be obvious that a potentially forbidden device is in use. There will be many interconnections between many data tools, almost all of which are out of sight or not obviously communicating. It will be impossible to control Bluetooth use by visual inspection.

The good part about the Bluetooth radio system is that although it may become ubiquitous, it has a very low transmit power level. These low power levels are not thought to be able to affect the systems on the airplane, which alleviates that very important concern.

Chapter 2: Technology Summary

Testing has actually begun with certain airlines to prove or disprove the safety of using Bluetooth wireless communication onboard an airline. It is anticipated that by the end of 2001, several airlines will approve the use of Bluetooth devices on airplanes while in flight. This would be helpful to airlines because it seems relatively unlikely that they could prevent the use of radio devices anyway.

Distances To Expect

How far will my Bluetooth enabled information tool reach? It depends, since your mileage may vary and your distance for Bluetooth wireless communications will also vary.

Distance is highly dependent on the local environment; the path from the access point to your computer and the reflectors (walls, people, equipment) in between. More on reflections later.

First, let's go outside and see how well the system works. Outdoors is the ideal environment: fresh air, direct paths called line-of-sight, sunshine, no walls to knock down the signal by 15 to 20 dB (See Chapter 4 for the information box "What is DBM?") Here the propagation path loss is approximately proportional to distance raised to the second power. So, if you both transmit 0 dBm and your receiver has a sensitivity of -85 dBm, you can walk as far away from the other unit as 85 dB will allow. Let's see, free-space path loss between two isotropic sources of unit gain is given by $32.4 + 20\log(f_{mhz}) + 20\log(d_{km})$. Oh, yes, it has an inverse square law dependence on frequency and distance, so in an open field, you can be 300 ft apart. But go inside your home and try to communicate through a 20 dB wall and your path loss now is 65 dB and the distance is only 30 ft.

Social Changes

It is still too early to determine exactly how Bluetooth wireless technology will change society and the people who are in it, but there are a few things that are worth thinking about. Ubiquitous connectivity and instant access to all information is going to make some excuses like, "I forgot that meeting," no longer credible.

This has some interesting ramifications. The effect of this new technology is actually somewhat surprising. It really brings people back to the type of relationships and the type of knowledge that they had when they lived and worked in small towns rather than in big cities. So, rather than having technological alienation, you instead have a closer "village" with the people whom you deal with every day.

Chapter 2: Technology Summary

Sharing the Air

Now here's a noble thought. We will "share the air." Let's say that I'm the only person at home and I am accessing the Internet through my Bluetooth connection. I settle into my leather couch, open my battery-powered web pad and up comes the Internet at 721 kbps (the best user-perceived **b**its **p**er **s**econd data rate for a Bluetooth connection). This is awesome. A few minutes later, my daughter comes home, says "Hi, Dad!" opens her web pad in the next room, and starts in with Instant Messenger, communicating through a second access point. Do I still have 721 kbps? Good question.

We know that if I only had one access point in my home that we'd share that 721 kbps in the same piconet. That is, I would get half the time slots and my daughter would get the other half. Of course, she would only be using Instant Messenger, so maybe I'd get 6 slots to every slot she gets, and my data rate experience would be 600 kbps, whereas she'd experience (and only need) 100 kbps. But what happens when we have two access points attached to a 1 Mbps connection? Wouldn't we both experience 721 kbps?

In an ideal world, yes. The actual situation is quite close. Say the two masters are asynchronous and have different hopping sequences. There are 79 possible channels, so the hit rate would be something like the probability that a slot overlaps another slot's time/frequency. This makes the slot vulnerability almost 3 slots wide. The random nature of the frequency use makes the likelihood of overlap about 3/79, or about 4%, degradation.

Chapter 2: Technology Summary

What about Wireless Local Area Networks?

In many ways Wireless Personal Area Networks™ are similar to Wireless Local Area Networks (WLANs). The differences are, well, kind of "personal."

WLANs were created with the idea that there is an existing wired infrastructure that would be very handy to hook up to without the bother of wiring or configuration problems. WLAN orientation is to reach outward and connect local devices to the world. At least some of the devices being interconnected are assumed to be non-moving or moving slowly or infrequently, thereby acting as fixed resources for the mobile members of the WLAN.

Technologies, such as those described in the Bluetooth Specification, have a different orientation. They establish and coordinate their own infrastructure. This infrastructure is assumed to float about, connecting and disconnecting objects as the need arises.

WLANs are essentially bridges. Bluetooth wireless technology is a communications bubble that moves with the user.

Chapter 3: Bluetooth Applications

Bluetooth Applications

> **Chapter 3**
> · Bluetooth Applications
> · Simple User Applications
> · A Complex Application

Most people don't buy technology. They buy solutions to their problems. If a Bluetooth product presents more problems than it solves, people won't buy it. Additionally, it is important to have instant user gratification. Bluetooth devices must be able to work right out of the box just as they are.

Simple User Applications

The Bluetooth SIG targeted several simple applications as a feasibility check during the creation and finalization of

> **Simple setup is the key**
>
> There is a problem with having a personal data tool that is purchased off-the-shelf. My device would be just like anybody else's device. It does not know who I am or what other devices I think are appropriate to exchange information with. It needs to be personalized. Out of the box there is no way that I can have pre-established control over who has access to my device. So, I have to have some certain amount of set up. It is very important that designers of user applications and data tools understand that the process of initialization and set up is critical to their success.
>
> **If it's not simple, no one but the early adopters of the technology will ever use it.**

the Specification. These applications have "lots of bang-for-the-buck" and arguably have large markets. The following lists the four premiere application areas for this new technology.

Simple applications of Bluetooth Wireless Technology	
3-in-1 phone	At home, your phone functions as a portable phone (fixed line charge). When you're on the move, it functions as a mobile phone (cellular charge). And when your phone comes within range of another mobile phone with built-in Bluetooth wireless technology, it functions as a walkie-talkie (no telephony charge).
The ultimate headset	Connect your wireless headset to your mobile phone, mobile computer, or any wired connection to keep your hands free for more important tasks when you're at the office or in your car.
The interactive conference	In meetings and conferences you can transfer selected documents instantly to selected participants, and exchange electronic business cards automatically, without any wired connections or the necessity of having to line up infrared beams.
The automatic synchronizer	Automatic synchronization of your desktop, mobile computer, notebook (PC-PDA and PC-HPC), and your mobile phone. For instance, as soon as you enter your office the address list and calendar in your notebook will automatically be updated to agree with the one in your desktop, or vice versa.

Chapter 3: Bluetooth Applications

Of course, all of the applications in the table would use the security features of the Bluetooth wireless technology to ensure that all personal information and correspondence remains confidential.

A Complex Application

Now that we've looked at some of the simpler uses of the Bluetooth wireless technology, what about the more complex, or in this case, a more compound example?

Consider the scenario where a busy executive receives an urgent email, reads it, replies to it, and sends the reply. Now, that's a pretty simple example, and it is something that is pretty easy to do when one is sitting at an information terminal. However, if one happens to be running through the airport at the time, it is considerably more difficult.

Bluetooth wireless technology helps to solve the problem of a non-ideal environment. The information transfer is done in the following way.

Chapter 3: Bluetooth Applications

• An executive running through the airport receives an email via her cell phone.

• The cell phone then relays that email to her Personal Digital Assistant (PDA).

• The PDA then changes the email into a voice mail. The PDA also inspects the email to determine whether or not it is urgent.

• Having determined that the email is indeed urgent, the PDA contacts the ear bud headset in the ear of the executive and transmits the voice version of the message. (The PDA, of course, asked the executive before interrupting her.)

• The executive acknowledges the voice mail and dictates a reply email.

• The message is then, in turn, transmitted to the PDA from the ear bud. The PDA then translates that voice into text, and then the cell phone sends the resultant email.

This whole process allows a busy person to be connected and to function in a way that is similar to that which could be done in an office. All of this is done through the use of Bluetooth wireless technology.

Chapter 3: Bluetooth Applications

It is not that any of these things *could not* be done right now if you used wires with the same devices in the same situation. It is just that it *would not* be done, because it would be too difficult to set up.

Bluetooth wireless technology gives people new capabilities and new possibilities for freeing themselves from being at any one particular geographic location.

Chapter 4: Section-By-Section Summary

Section-By-Section Summary

The various parts of the Bluetooth Specification were written at different times, in different places, and by different authors. Not surprisingly, they have varying degrees of introductory and support material. This chapter gives you a picture of each part and sub-part. It can be used as a guide to help determine which sections are of the most

> Chapter 4
> · Radio
> · Baseband
> · LMP
> · L2CAP
> · SDP
> · RFCOMM
> · HCI
> · Profiles
> · Appendices

interest to you. These snapshots also relate the material in each part with other components of the Specification.

... at a Glance

Function: Concise description of the primary role this function plays in the Bluetooth protocol stack

Part: Section letter of the Specification

Interfaces: Which other function block interacts with this block

Chapter 4: Section-By-Section Summary

Radio

> ### *Radio at a Glance*
> **Function**: Send and receive bits over the air and process information from and to the protocol layers above
>
> **Part**: A
>
> **Interfaces**: Air, Baseband

The Bluetooth radio is the foundation of the technology. It is what makes all of the protocols above it useful. Part A, the section on the radio, is the shortest of the sections of the Bluetooth Specification. The radio operates in what the USA calls the Industrial, Scientific, Medical (ISM) band. A band such as this has been set aside by most of the countries in the world to allow for the free exchange of information in unlicensed form. This is in contrast to other radio systems, such as cellular phones, which are licensed; someone owns that air space. No one actually owns the ISM bands. These bands are not uniformly allocated across the world. Almost all countries have something like ISM bands in the general area of 2.4 GHz. However, some of them are wider and some of them are narrower in terms of the number of megahertz that the band has been allocated. Historically, countries such as Japan, France, and Spain have had narrower allocations. However, recently those countries have begun to move toward a more unified approach.

The ISM band itself is generally about 80 MHz wide.

Chapter 4: Section-By-Section Summary

Bluetooth protocol chops this up into about 79 individual channels, with a little bit of guard band on each side. This makes channels that are about 1 MHz wide.

The radio is told by the Baseband layer to transmit a Gaussian frequency shift keying (GFSK) modulation at a symbol rate of 1 Mbps on one of the 1 MHz channels. Basically, two tones are used: center frequency plus 500 kHz represents a one (1), and center frequency minus 500 kHz is a zero (0).

The Radio section of the Specification, often referred to as RF, has five subsections of interest:

    1) Scope
    2) Frequency Band and Channel Arrangement
    3) Transmitter Characteristics
    4) Receiver Characteristics
    5) Testing Parameters

Radio—Scope

This is where you go if you want to know who regulates the airwaves where you live. This is likely the most out-of-date section, since governments tend to change this information frequently. It is best to consult your local country regulatory body.

Chapter 4: Section-By-Section Summary

Radio—Frequency Band and Channel Arrangement

As mentioned in the introduction, the Bluetooth system operates in the 2.4 GHz band. In a vast majority of countries around the world, the range of this frequency band is 2400-2483.5 MHz. This range is generally called *microwaves*.

Time is divided into 625 µs intervals called slots where a different RF channel is used for each slot. This gives a nominal hop rate of 1600 hops/sec. One short packet can be transmitted per interval/slot. Alternate slots are used for transmitting and receiving from the unit that controls transmissions, which results in a Time-Division Duplex (TDD) scheme.

Microwaves?
...as in Microwave ovens?

Yes, 2.4 GHz radiation is what cooks popcorn. Before you become concerned, the level of power for the Bluetooth radio is much, much less than that of a microwave oven. A typical microwave oven is somewhere between 600 W and 900 W. The typical Bluetooth device will be less than 100 mW, and often less than 10 mW. The power levels are, obviously, several orders of magnitude apart. In fact, the leakage from a normal microwave oven is probably 10 to 100 times greater than any Bluetooth device will ever be.

Chapter 4: Section-By-Section Summary

Radio—Transmitter Characteristics

The equipment is classified into three power classes as follows:

Power class	Maximum output power (P_{max})	Nominal output power	Maximum output power[1]	Power control
1	100 mW (20 dBm)	N/A	1 mW (0 dBm)	P_{min} < +4 dBm to P_{max} optional: P_{min}2 to P_{max}
2	2.5 mW (4 dBm)	1 mW (0 dBm)	0.25 mW (-6 dBm)	Optional: P_{min}2 to P_{max}
3	1 mW (0 dBm)	N/A	N/A	Optional: P_{min}2 to P_{max}

Note 1—Minimum output power at maximum power setting.
Note 2—The lower power limit P_{min} < -30 dBm is suggested, but is not mandatory, and may be chosen according to application needs.

Radio—Receiver Characteristics

Receivers are typically defined in terms of sensitivity. The sensitivity level for Bluetooth wireless technology is defined as the input level for which a raw bit error rate (BER) of 0.1% is met. The requirement for a Bluetooth receiver is an actual sensitivity level of -70 dBm or better. The receiver must achieve the -70 dBm sensitivity level

Chapter 4: Section-By-Section Summary

with any Bluetooth transmitter compliant to the transmitter specified in the Transmitter section.

> **What is a dBm?**
>
> Before we answer that question, we must know what a dB is. The abbreviation dB is for decibel, a *relative* measure given by ten times the log of a relative linear number. For instance, if window air conditioner #1 was measured to be twice as loud as air conditioner #2, then the log (base 10) of #2 is 0.301 and #1 is 3 dB louder than #2.
>
> Now, what's a dBm? This is the *absolute* measure of power, referenced to a milliwatt. More specifically, the thousandth of a watt was measured in an impedance system of nominally 50 Ω (most common RF equipment). To give you a feel for the range of values for dBm, -100 dBm is a tenth of a nano-watt (the sensitivity of a cellular phone receiver), 0 dBm is 1 mW (Class 3 Bluetooth transmitter maximum), 20 dBm is 100 mW (Class 1 Bluetooth transmitter maximum), and 30 dBm is a watt (about the power supplied by a cell phone charger). Things move along pretty quickly when you talk in dBs, don't they? Go ask your boss for "only" a 3 dB salary increase and see what happens!

Radio—Testing Parameters

The testing parameters are outlined in the appendixes to the Radio. These descriptions are interesting, but do not outline procedures to fully test the Radios. In fact, these tests refer only to the required operational characteristics such as operating temperatures and voltage requirements.

Chapter 4: Section-By-Section Summary

Formal testing specifications are available to those who wish to qualify their products to have the Bluetooth logo. You must be part of the Bluetooth Special Interest Group as an Adopter, Associate, or Promoter to get these specifications. See the description of the Bluetooth Special Interest Group in Chapter 6 for more information on the various levels of membership.

Baseband

This is one of the largest and most complex parts of the Specification. The Baseband Layer defines and controls the frequency-hop/time-division-duplex (FH/TDD) method of controlling the radio's transmissions. It does much more than the traditional role that the Baseband function plays in the cellular telephone world.

> *Baseband at a Glance*
>
> **Function**: Control the radio and change the bits to radio packets (and back). This includes a low-level routing of information to higher-level protocols.
>
> **Part**: B
>
> **Interfaces**: Radio, LMP, L2CAP, Audio

Bluetooth Baseband section describes 14 areas:

1) General Description of Baseband
2) Physical Channel
3) Physical Links
4) Packet Formats
5) Error Correction

Chapter 4: Section-By-Section Summary

6) Logical Channels
7) Data Whitening
8) Transmit/Receive Routines
9) Transmit/Receive Timing
10) Channel Control
11) Hop Selection
12) Audio Interface
13) Device Addressing
14) Security

The Traditional Role of Baseband

Baseband is another way of saying modulation and de-modulation. Why modulation? Two reasons: 1) the natural interferers to communication are impulse-like and 2) we'd like to cram as much digital information as possible into a hertz of bandwidth. One could directly amplitude modulate the digital information. This is done in AM radio and produces one cycle of music or speech for every cycle of RF bandwidth. It also allows crackling (lightning) and popping (man-made interference) to interfere with the communications. The first step away from interference is to modulate in another domain, like phase or frequency. Frequency Modulation (FM) comes to mind. No cracks and pops, and the 20 kHz of music is spread across 200 kHz of bandwidth, giving even more gain against interference. Of course, this does not use the bandwidth efficiently, but it sounds good!

In Bluetooth wireless technology, the digital information is modulated by 2-Frequency Shift Keying (FSK) (with a modulation index of 0.32) which has the property that one bit of data is transmitted in every cycle. This enables the highest data rates for reasonable implementation cost.

Chapter 4: Section-By-Section Summary

Baseband—General Description

The General Description of the Baseband turns out to be a pretty good general description of piconets and of the Bluetooth technology as a whole. It presents Bluetooth communications as a short-range radio link intended to replace the cable(s) connecting portable and/or fixed electronic devices.

The General Description does restate some of the attributes of the Radio. Since this rendition is brief it may be somewhat misleading. The best bet is to ignore the parts about the Radio and concentrate on the topology description, which is the relationship between the Bluetooth devices.

A Bluetooth piconet is the network formed by a master and one or more slaves. Each piconet is defined by a different frequency hopping sequence (or pattern) which becomes a physical channel based on the address and clock of the master station. All active units participating in the same piconet are synchronized to this channel.

It is very important to understand the topology of the Bluetooth system. Bluetooth wireless technology is said to provide a point-to-point connection (only two Bluetooth units involved in a piconet). In fact, it is just a sparsely populated master/slave setup; the two entities are not equals. The point-to-multipoint connection is a minor variation on the single slave. The slaves involved do not comprehend that there is anyone else talking to the master. Slaves are the ultimate "good children," they only speak when spoken to.

Where things get interesting is in the scatternet situation. Figure 4 shows a slave maintaining a relationship with two masters, which is explicitly supported by the Spec. It also shows two masters maintaining a relationship—the Spec is silent on details about this. How do you remain a "good child" (a slave) in one setting while being the boss of another group?

Physical Channels: like on your TV (sort of)

TV technology allocates a fixed portion of the RF spectrum for each of the broadcast streams that we call "channels." TV signals occupy a good portion of the spectrum allocated for each stream in a more-or-less homogenous way.

Bluetooth technology uses a different scheme for utilizing its shared allocation of the spectrum (its band). It uses Frequency Hopping Spread Spectrum, which is a way of saying that only a small amount of the available bandwidth is used at any one time (the Spread Spectrum part). It does this by slicing up the band into smaller bands and using them one at a time in a seemingly random manner (the Frequency Hopping part).

Chapter 4: Section-By-Section Summary

The thing that complicates this even more is that piconets are not allowed to be time or frequency synchronized. Each piconet has its own hopping sequence. The sequence is determined by the identity of the piconet master, and phase is determined by the master unit's system clock.

Another aspect of the piconet is also introduced here. A maximum of seven slaves can be **active** in the piconet. Many more slaves can remain locked to the master, ready to jump in while in a "parked state." There is a more complete discussion about this in the section on Channel Control, page 55.

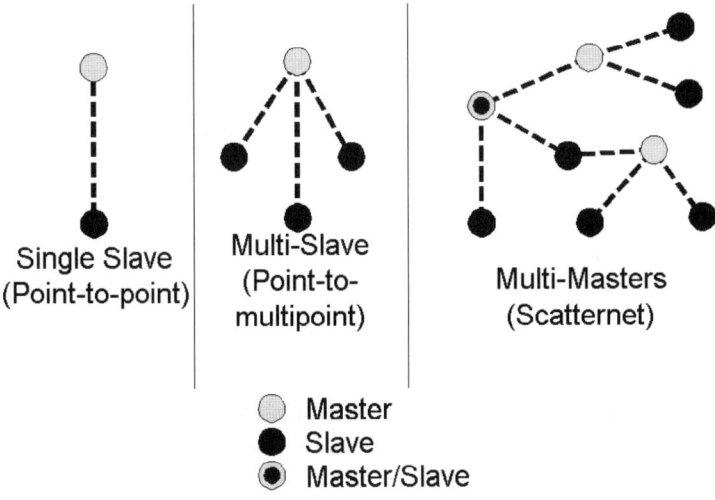

Figure 4—Slave/master relationships

Chapter 4: Section-By-Section Summary

Baseband—Physical Channel

The discussion of Channel Definition and Time Slots is very useful, and is the major reason for reading this subsection. It should be kept in mind that the Physical Channel is how the airwaves are used. The Physical Link (covered next) is what goes over that channel in terms of data streams.

Once again there is some overlap with the Radio section in this part. You can basically ignore the discussion of the Frequency Band and RF Channels along with Modulation and Bit Rate part.

Baseband—Physical Link

This section presents the two styles of communications in the Bluetooth wireless technology. They are two different kinds of physical links, each with their corresponding baseband packets (more about that later in **Packet Formats,** page 49).

- Synchronous Connection-Oriented (SCO) links carry time-critical information, and contain audio or a combination of audio and data.

- Asynchronous Connectionless (ACL) links are used for data only, and are transmitted on an as-time-permits basis.

Chapter 4: Section-By-Section Summary

The two types can be multiplexed on the same RF (Physical Channel) link. The Baseband gets and puts this to a single interface in the Radio, but interfaces to the Audio or LMP functions, as appropriate, based on the physical link specified in the packet.

Baseband—Packet Formats

Here is where the nuts and bolts of what gets transmitted over the air is defined. After the general format and syntax of the notation is explained, the derivation of the Access Code and Header is presented. Then each Baseband packet type is detailed. Figure 5 shows the general format of the Baseband Packet.

The Packet Summary in section 4.6 of the Bluetooth Specification is well worth a bookmark; you will likely refer to it often.

One of the things the table in the Specification does not do is give the meaning of the acronym. Table 2 will provide these

> **The Importance of Packet Formats**
>
> Having a good grasp of the various kinds and flavors of Bluetooth packets is essential for understanding much of what follows in the Bluetooth Spec.
>
> In addition to specifying how packets are constructed, the Packet Formats section also tells how the various packets are used. You can't just skim this section and come back when you want to know the format of a particular packet. You might not choose the right packet at all without careful attention to this section.

acronyms, and aid in reading the rest of this Guide, as well as the Specification.

Table 2

Acronym	Meaning
ID	Identification
NULL	Empty
POLL	Polling
FHS	Frequency Hopping Synchronization
DM1	Data—Medium Rate, single slot
DH1	Data—High Rate, single slot
DM3	Data—Medium Rate, three slots
DH3	Data—High Rate, three slots
DM5	Data—Medium Rate, five slots
DH5	Data—High Rate, five slots
AUX1	Auxiliary packet, one slot
HV1	High Quality Voice, one slot
HV2	High Quality Voice, two slots
HV3	High Quality Voice, three slots
DV	Data Voice

Chapter 4: Section-By-Section Summary

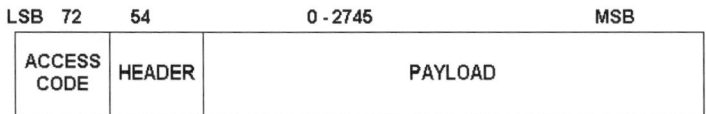

Figure 5—General format of Bluetooth baseband packets

Baseband—Error Correction

Both ACL (data) and SCO (audio and data) packets can be provided with different levels of Forward Error Correction (FEC) or Cyclic Redundancy Check (CRC) error correction and can be encrypted. Several schemes are defined here, along with what can be done to which kind of packet.

There are three error correction schemes defined for Bluetooth wireless communications:

- 1/3 rate FEC
- 2/3 rate FEC
- Automatic Repeat reQuest (ARQ) scheme

The purpose of the FEC scheme on the data payload is to reduce the number of retransmissions by making it possible to drop a few bits, while being able to recover the data. The Specification points out, however, that in a reasonably error-free environment, FEC is unnecessary overhead that reduces the throughput. Therefore, the packet definitions given later in the Specification make use of FEC in the payload an option, based on packet type. The packet header is always protected by a 1/3 rate FEC, since it contains valuable link information and must be able to sustain some bit errors.

Baseband—Logical Channels

Logical channels are an embellishment of the Physical Links. The five Bluetooth logical channels are defined in this section.

- LC control channel
- LM control channel
- UA user channel
- UI user channel
- US user channel

The paragraphs describing their use are somewhat convoluted, so Table 3 is provided for reference.

Chapter 4: Section-By-Section Summary

Table 3

Name	Type	Function	Location	Occurance
LC	Control	Link control	Header	All packets
LM	Control	Link management	Payload	SCO or ACL
UA	User	Asynchronous data	Payload	ACL or SCO-DV
UI	User	Isochronous data	Payload	ACL or SCO-DV
US	User	Synchronous data	Payload	SCO

Baseband—Data Whitening

Information carried via radio energy is easier to pluck out of the air if the data is more or less alternating ones and zeros. Modulations are easier to catch than a monotone. Since data is often monotonous, something needs to be done to make it more interesting. That something is "Whitening."

Whitening is the process of taking perfectly good headers and data and scrambling them to make them easier to receive (which is the hard part of radio technology, in case you didn't know). The trick, then, is to get the original data back. This section describes how both things are done.

Chapter 4: Section-By-Section Summary

Baseband—Transmit/Receive Routines

This section describes one way, perhaps not the best way, to use the packets defined in the Packet Formats section to perform transmits and receives.

ACL, SCO, and combined ACL/SCO streams are discussed. The information presented here gives you another chance to understand the concepts presented in Packet Formats.

Baseband—Transmit/Receive Timing

Timing is of the essence. This section describes the timing tolerances of the Bluetooth system. It also describes in some detail the master/slave timing relationship. The best representation of how piconet timing, and the orderly interchange of data, works is in Figure 9.7 of the Specification. As with many of the illustrations in the Spec, the figure fully describes the interactions, but suffers from a lack of labeling. Figure 6 shows the same set of interchanges, but with more explanation.

The master always transmits on even numbered slots. The slave that was just addressed must respond in the next (odd) slot. Slaves should always listen on the even slots, because they never know when they might be addressed.

Chapter 4: Section-By-Section Summary

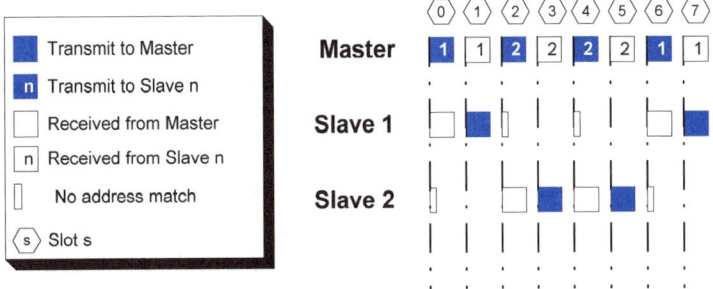

Figure 6—Multi-slave operation

Baseband—Channel Control

The details of how piconets are organized and maintained are covered in this section. A description of how the channel of a piconet is established and how units can be added to and released from the piconet is given. Nine states of operation of the Bluetooth units are defined to support these functions. In addition, the operation of the scatternet is discussed.

The channel in the piconet is defined by the operational characteristics of the master of the piconet. The hopping sequence and the channel access codes are derived from the system clock and device ID of the master.

The text specifies that the names "master" and "slave" only refer to the protocol on the channel. Bluetooth units are defined to be functionally identical. Any Bluetooth device can become a master of a piconet; there are no "slave-only" devices. Further, once a piconet has been established, master-slave roles can be exchanged.

Table 4 shows the different states used in the Bluetooth link controller. There are two major states (STANDBY and CONNECTION) and seven substates, which are interim states that are used to add new slaves to a piconet.

Baseband—Hop Selection

The section on Channel Control alluded to various kinds of hopping sequences for changing states. These different kinds are necessary if masters and slaves are ever going to connect. Consider that if both a master and a slave picked the same hopping sequence at the same hopping rate, they might never coincide.

Ten types of hopping sequences are defined: five for the 79-hop system and five for the 23-hop system (shown in parentheses), respectively. These sequences are as follows:

- A **page hopping sequence** with 32 (16) unique wake-up frequencies distributed equally over the 79 (23) MHz, with a period length of 32 (16).
- A **page response sequence** covering 32 (16) unique response frequencies that have a one-to-one correspondence to the current page hopping sequence.

Chapter 4: Section-By-Section Summary

Table 4

State	Description
STANDBY	This is the default state in the Bluetooth unit where it is in a low-power mode and not actively communicating (not a part of a piconet).
CONNECTION	After the connection has been established, packets can be sent back and forth.
page	The substate that is used by the master to activate and connect to a slave that periodically wakes up in the **page scan** substate.
page scan	A potential slave listens for its device access code for a set duration. The unit listens at a single hop frequency long enough to completely scan 16 page frequencies.
inquiry	Similar to the **page** substate, this substate is used by a master to discover a set of new devices. The master does not acknowledge the inquiry response messages, but keeps probing at different hop channels and, in between, listens for response packets.
inquiry scan	Similar to the **page scan** substate. However, in this substate, a potential slave looks for its inquiry access code instead of its address.
master response	The master enters this substate when it receives a reply from the slave after it has been **page**d.
slave response	On recognizing its device access code, the slave enters this substate.
inquiry response	On recognizing its inquiry access code, the device enters this substate.

- An **inquiry sequence** with 32 (16) unique wake-up frequencies distributed equally over the 79 (23) MHz, with a period length of 32 (16).

- An **inquiry response sequence** covering 32 (16) unique response frequencies that have a one-to-one correspondence to the current inquiry hopping sequence.

- A **channel hopping sequence** which has a very long period length. It does not show repetitive patterns over a short time interval, but rather distributes the hop frequencies equally over the 79 (23) MHz during a short time interval.

Baseband—Audio Interface

Audio in Bluetooth wireless technology is handled much like audio in cell phones—it is coded on the transmit side and decoded to an approximation of the original on the receive side.

Bluetooth audio is coded in one of two ways: 8-bit logarithmic or linear. The appropriate voice-coding scheme is selected after negotiations between the Link Managers of the two units involved.

Chapter 4: Section-By-Section Summary

The 8-bit coding is a 64 kbps log Pulse Coded Modulation (PCM) format using A-law or µ-law compression. Under ideal conditions, this format can be used effectively. The compression method follows ITU-T recommendations G. 711.

The linear coding is 64 kbps Continuous Variable Slope Delta (CVSD) Modulation, which provides a more robust format for voice over the air interface.

In both cases, the "audio" is assumed to be a telephone-quality voice interaction, not an audio stream such as would support MP3.

Baseband—Device Addressing

Each Bluetooth transceiver is allocated a unique 48-bit Bluetooth device address (BD_ADDR). This address is assigned by the IEEE Registration Authority (http://standards.ieee.org/regauth/oui/index.shtml) to manufacturers and is called an Organizationally Unique Identifier (OUI).

The OUI is defined in IEEE Std 802-1990 and is used to generate 48 bit Universal LAN MAC addresses to identify LAN and MAN stations uniquely, and to generate Protocol Identifiers to identify public and private protocols.

Bluetooth communications uses this 48-bit address to cre-

Chapter 4: Section-By-Section Summary

ate its own format. The OUI is divided into three fields (see Figure 7) as follows:

- LAP field: lower address part consisting of 24 bits
- UAP field: upper address part consisting of 8 bits
- NAP field: nonsignificant address part consisting of 16 bits

The LAP and UAP form the significant part of the BD_ADDR. The total address space is 2^{32}.

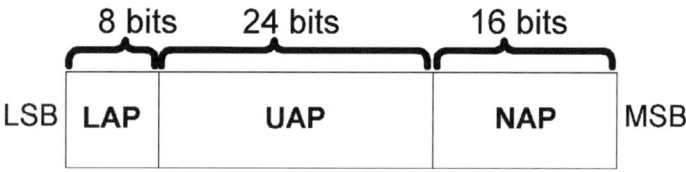

Figure 7—Bluetooth address format

Baseband—Security

Bluetooth wireless communications provide peer-to-peer communications over the air. In theory, anyone could listen in to the interchange, but most people don't like that idea. In order to provide some protection and information confidentiality, the system provides security measures both at the application layer and the link layer. All Bluetooth authentication and encryption routines are implemented in the same way.

Four different entities are used for maintaining security at the link layer: a unique public address for each user, two secret keys, and a random number that is different for each transaction.

Entities used in authentication and encryption procedures	
Entity	**Size**
Unique Bluetooth device address (BD_ADDR)	48 bits
Private user key, authentication	128 bits
Private user key for encryption that is configurable in length in increments of 8 bytes (byte-wise)	8-128 bits
Random number (RAND)	128 bits

The secret keys are derived during initialization and are never again exchanged during the life of the piconet. The encryption key is derived from the authentication key during the authentication process. The authentication algorithm always uses 128 bits.

For the encryption algorithm, the key size may vary between 1 octet and 16 octets (8-128 bits). The size of the encryption key is configurable for two reasons.

1) To comply with differences in requirements imposed on cryptographic algorithms in different countries.

2) To provide a future upgrade path for the security without the need of a costly redesign of the algorithms and encryption hardware. Increasing the key size is the simplest way to combat increased computing power of potential eavesdroppers.

LMP

The Link Manager Protocol (LMP) section describes the procedures used to set up and maintain pathways of communication between Bluetooth devices. It is the "housekeeping" part of the protocol. LMP packets contain no user data.

> *LMP at a Glance*
> **Function**: Manage the relationship between Bluetooth units
>
> **Part**: D
>
> **Interfaces**: Baseband, L2CAP, HCI

The LMP part covers seven areas of interest as follows:

1) General Overview
2) Format of LMP Messages
3) Procedure Rules and Protocol Data Unit Definitions

4) Connection Establishment
5) A Summary of PDUs
6) Test Modes
7) Error Handling

LMP—General Overview

This one-page overview provides a good summary of the purpose of the LMP. It talks about the concept of the Link Manager (LM) and Link Controller (LC), but does not mention specifically that those entities are not formally defined in the Specification.

It is important to remember that the subject of this section is the conversation between a pair of LMs, not about the LMs themselves. The behavior of the LM is described, but not the internal details. The details of the internal workings are left to the implementers.

LMP—Format of LMP Messages

The LM's Protocol Data Units (PDUs) are always sent as single-slot packets and the payload header is 1 byte. The two least significant bits in the payload header determine the logical channel. For LM PDUs these bits are set to 11 (binary) (see Figure 8).

Chapter 4: Section-By-Section Summary

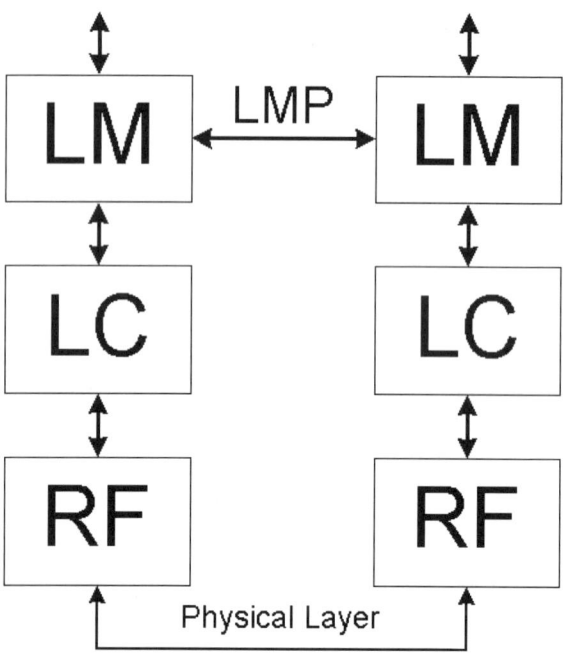

Figure 8—LMP, LM, and LC

LMP—Procedure Rules and Protocol Data Unit Definitions

This section is key for people who implement the lower layers of the Bluetooth protocol. It explains the mechanism of participation in a piconet in great detail. Table 5 highlights the procedures covered.

Chapter 4: Section-By-Section Summary

Table 5

Procedure	Use
General Response Messages	Used to tell the originator of a request or command whether or not the command was accepted—and presumably acted upon.
Authentication	The authentication procedure is based on a challenge-response scheme to validate potential members of a piconet
Pairing	This is used when two devices do not have a common link key or an initialization key. This procedure creates one based on a Personal Identification Number (PIN) and a random number
Change link key	If two devices are paired and the link key is derived from combination keys, the link can be changed to enhance security.
Change the current link key	The current link key can be a semi-permanent link key or a temporary link key. Changing to a temporary link key is necessary if the piconet is to support encrypted broadcast, which would then allow a common link key for all members of the piconet.
Encryption	This starts the encryption process. Encryption may be used if at least one authentication has been performed.

Chapter 4: Section-By-Section Summary

Table 5 *(continued)*

Procedure	Use
Clock offset request	When a slave receives the FHS packet, the difference is always computed between its own clock and the master's clock. This request causes the slave to include that calculation in the payload of the FHS packet, so the master knows on what RF channel the slave wakes up to PAGE SCAN after it has left the piconet.
Slot offset information	Response to **Clock offset request.**
Timing accuracy information request	The timing accuracy parameters returned are the long-term drift measured in parts per million (ppm) and the long term jitter measured in milliseconds (ms) of the clock. They are used during hold, sniff, and park modes. These parameters are fixed for a certain device and must be identical every time it is requested.
LMP version	Request for the version of the LM protocol.
Supported features	The radio and link controller packet types and features subset supported by this unit are returned as a result of this request.
Switch of master-slave role	Since the paging device always becomes the master of the piconet, a switch of the master-slave role is sometimes needed.
Name request	Request for the user-friendly name associated with the Bluetooth device. This name must consist of a maximum of 248 bytes coded according to the UTF-8 standard.

Chapter 4: Section-By-Section Summary

Table 5 *(continued)*

Procedure	Use
Detach	Terminates the connection between two Bluetooth devices. This may be done anytime by either the master or the slave. A Reason parameter is included in the message to inform the other party of why the connection is closed.
Hold mode	The link between two Bluetooth devices can be placed in hold mode for a specified time. During this time, no ACL packets will be transmitted from the master.
Sniff mode	Switches to a low duty cycle mode where the slave is not expected to answer at all times. When the link is in sniff mode, the master can only start a transmission in the negotiated sniff slot.
Park mode	If a slave does not need to participate in the channel, but still should be FH-synchronized, it can be placed in park mode. In this mode, the device gives up its place in the piconet, but still resynchronizes to the channel by waking up at the beacon instants separated by the beacon interval.
Power control	If the Receive Signal Strength Indication (RSSI) value differs too much from the preferred value of a Bluetooth device, it can request an increase or a decrease of the other device's transmit power. Upon receipt of this message, the output power is increased or decreased one step.

Table 5 *(continued)*

Procedure	Use
Channel quality-driven change between DM and DH	A device is configured to always use DM (Data Medium rate, protected with a 2/3 FEC code) packets, to always use DH (Data High rate, not protected) packets, or to automatically adjust its packet type according to the quality of the channel. This command sets the latter.
Quality of service (QoS)	A poll interval, which is defined as the maximum time between subsequent transmissions from the master to a particular slave, is set by this command. The poll interval is somewhat guaranteed. The exceptions are when there are collisions with page, page scan, inquiry, and inquiry scan.
SCO links	Establishes the SCO link, which reserves regular time slots for data exchange between units. The length of time between these slots is called the SCO interval.
Control of multi-slot packets	The number of slots used by a slave in its return packet can be limited. The master allows the slave to use a maximal number of slots through this procedure.
Paging scheme	Sets one of the optional paging schemes, which is to be used the next time a unit is paged.
Link supervision	This LMP procedure is used to set the value of the supervision timeout for monitoring the existence of the link.

Chapter 4: Section-By-Section Summary

LMP—Connection Establishment

When the paging device wishes to create a connection involving layers above LM, it sends the LM a request to connect to the host. When the other side receives this message, the host is informed about the incoming connection. The remote device can accept or reject the connection request. After connection is established, the first packet on a logical channel different from LMP can then be transmitted.

LMP—A Summary of PDUs

This is a more comprehensive table than is included in this Guide. It is good reference material, worthy of a bookmark.

LMP—Test Modes

The LMP has PDUs to support different Bluetooth test modes, which are used for certification and compliance testing of the Bluetooth Radio and Baseband. Sending a test mode command to the LM to the device under test (DUT) activates this mode. The DUT is always the slave. The LM must be able to receive this message anytime. When the DUT has entered test mode, an LMP command is sent to the DUT to start a specific test.

LMP—Error Handling

If the LM receives a PDU with unrecognized opcode, it rejects it. The unrecognized opcode is echoed back in a reply PDU's parameter. If the LM receives a PDU with invalid parameters, it responds with a rejection with the reason code "invalid LMP parameters."

If the maximum response time is exceeded or if a link loss is detected, the party that waits for the response will conclude that the procedure has terminated unsuccessfully.

Since LMP PDUs are not interpreted in real time, collision situations can occur where both LMs initiate the same procedure and both cannot be completed. In this situation, the master rejects the slave-initiated procedure with the reason code "LMP Error Transaction Collision." The master-initiated procedure will then be completed.

L2CAP

The Logical Link Control and Adaption Protocol (L2CAP) specification is responsible for providing connection-oriented and connectionless data services to upper layer protocols. It has protocol multiplexing

> *L2CAP at a Glance*
> **Function**: Provide connection-oriented and connectionless data services to upper-layer protocols not involving Audio
>
> **Part**: D
>
> **Interfaces**: Baseband, LMP, all higher-level protocols

capability, along with segmentation and reassembly of large user data packets. L2CAP permits higher-level protocols and applications to transmit and receive L2CAP data packets up to 64 kilobytes in length. It also supports the concept of group abstractions.

There are nine sections of interest in the L2CAP part:
- 1) Introduction
- 2) General Operation
- 3) State Machine
- 4) Data Packet Format
- 5) Signaling
- 6) Configuration Parameter Options
- 7) Service Primitives
- 8) Configuration Message Sequence Charts
- 9) Implementation Guidelines

L2CAP—Introduction

This section of the Bluetooth Specification overviews the Logical Link Control and Adaption (not Adaptation, as is sometimes cited in the press) Protocol, referred to as L2CAP (pronounced "el two cap"). L2CAP is layered over the Baseband Protocol and resides in the data link layer. L2CAP provides the following:

- Connection-oriented and connectionless data services to upper layer protocols

- Protocol multiplexing
- Segmentation and reassembly
- Group abstractions

The L2CAP Specification is defined for only Asynchronous Connection-Less (ACL) links, and no support for Synchronous Connection-Oriented (SCO) links is provided. ACL links support best effort traffic. Since L2CAP depends on integrity checks in the Baseband to protect the transmitted information, AUX1 packets are never allowed to transport L2CAP packets. L2CAP permits higher-level protocols and applications to transmit and receive L2CAP data packets up to 64 kilobytes in length.

L2CAP supports protocol multiplexing because the Baseband Protocol does not support any "type" field identifying the higher layer protocol being multiplexed above it. Baseband only multiplexes the SCO and ACL streams. L2CAP must distinguish between upper layer protocols such as the Service Discovery Protocol, RFCOMM, and Telephony Control.

The Segmentation and Reassembly (SAR) functionality is absolutely necessary to support protocols using packets larger than those supported by the Baseband. Compared to wired physical media, the data packets defined by the Baseband Protocol are limited in size. Limiting higher layer protocols to the maximum transmission unit (MTU) size associated with the largest Baseband payload (341 bytes for DH5 packets) limits their efficiency. The higher level protocols are generally designed to use larger packets. Large packets sent to L2CAP are segmented into multiple smaller Baseband packets prior to their transmission over the air. Similarly, multiple received Baseband packets are reassembled into a single larger L2CAP packet following a simple integrity check.

Many protocols include the concept of a group of addresses. The Baseband Protocol supports the concept of a piconet, a group of devices synchronously hopping together using the same clock. The L2CAP group abstraction permits implementations to efficiently map protocol groups on to piconets. Without a group abstraction, higher-level protocols would need to be exposed to the Baseband Protocol and Link Manager functionality in order to manage groups efficiently.

L2CAP—General Operation

L2CAP is based around the concept of "channels." The Channel identifier (CID) defines its use. The CID is simply an endpoint used to demultiplex the incoming packet.

Connection-oriented data channels represent a connection between two devices, where a CID identifies each endpoint of the channel. The connectionless channels restrict data flow to a single direction. These channels are used to support a channel "group" where the CID on the source represents one or more remote devices. There are also a number of CIDs reserved for special purposes. The signaling channel is one example of a reserved channel.

L2CAP—State Machine

This section describes the L2CAP connection-oriented channel state machine. The section defines the states, the events causing state transitions, and the actions to be performed in response to events. This state machine is only pertinent to bi-directional CIDs and is not representative of the signaling channel or the unidirectional channel.

L2CAP is packet based, but follows a communication model based on channels. A channel represents a data flow between L2CAP entities in remote devices. Channels may be connection oriented or connectionless. All packet fields use Little Endian byte order.

L2CAP—Data Packet Format

The connection-oriented data packets are used to support a reliable point-to-point conversation, not SCO links as one might guess. The connectionless data packets support nonreliable group communications, sometimes called multicast. Table 6 shows the types of L2CAP Data Packets.

Table 6—Data packet types

CID	Description
0x0000	Null identifier
0x0001	Signaling channel
0x0002	Connectionless reception channel
0x0003-0x003F	Reserved
0x0040-0xFFFF	Dynamically allocated

L2CAP—Signaling

The signaling commands passed between two L2CAP entities on remote devices are documented here. All signaling commands are sent to CID 0x0001. The L2CAP implementation must be able to determine the Bluetooth address of the device that sent the commands. Multiple commands may be sent in a single (L2CAP) packet.

Maximum Transmission Unit (MTU) Commands take the form of Requests and Responses. All L2CAP implementations support the reception of signaling packets whose MTU does not exceed 48 bytes. L2CAP implementations should not use signaling packets beyond this size without first testing whether the implementation can support larger signaling packets.

L2CAP—Configuration Parameter Options

Options are a mechanism to extend the ability to negotiate different connection requirements. Options are transmitted in the form of information elements comprised of an option type, an option length, and of one or more option data fields.

The types are as follows:
- Maximum Transmission Unit (MTU)
- Flush Timeout Option
- Quality of Service (QoS) Option

L2CAP—Service Primitives

This section presents an abstract description of the services offered by L2CAP in terms of service primitives and parameters. The service interface is required for testing. The interface is described independently of any platform-specific implementation. All data values use Little Endian byte ordering.

L2CAP—Configuration Message Sequence Charts

The examples in this appendix describe a sample of the many possible configuration scenarios that might occur. Currently, these are provided as suggestions and may change in the next update of the Specification.

Chapter 4: Section-By-Section Summary

L2CAP—Implementation Guidelines

This section contains some guidelines for implementations. These guidelines are not part of the compliance tests. They are simply suggestions on how to solve (or avoid) some difficult problems.

SDP

The Service Discovery Protocol (SDP) is the mechanism whereby Bluetooth devices discover which services are available and the characteristics of those services.

> **SDP at a Glance**
>
> **Function**: Allows Bluetooth devices to find out what they can do with other Bluetooth devices
>
> **Part**: E
>
> **Interfaces:** L2CAP, Higher layer protocols

The term "services" includes a broad range of applications or resources. Common applications include printing, paging, and faxing. Access to resources may include information access to servers or service providers. Part of the function of SDP is to provide the means of finding and obtaining the protocols, access methods, "drivers," and other code necessary to utilize the service. Other attributes are also controlled through this protocol, such as controlling access to the services, advertising your services to others, choosing among competing services, billing for services, and similar things.

The sections of interest in SDP are as follows:

> 1) Introduction
> 2) Overview
> 3) Data Representation
> 4) Protocol Description
> 5) Service Attribute Definitions
> 6) Background Information
> 7) Example SDP Transactions

SDP—Introduction

The SDP mechanism provides the means for client applications to discover the existence of services and their attributes provided by server applications.

SDP—Overview

The attributes of a service include the type or class of service offered (protocol description) and information about mechanism or protocol (data representation) information needed to utilize the service. This part of the Specification documents the mechanics of how service discovery works.

Chapter 4: Section-By-Section Summary

SDP—Data Representation

The data representations of attributes are formalized lists of primitives, called elements. SDP defines a simple mechanism to describe the attribute values of various types with arbitrary complexity. The SDP attribute list construct is generally useful across a wide variety of service classes and environments.

SDP—Protocol Description

SDP is a simple protocol with minimal requirements on the underlying transport. SDP uses a request/response model where each transaction consists of one request PDU and one response PDU. There is no guarantee, however, that a series of requests will result in the return of responses in the same order.

When SDP utilizes the Bluetooth L2CAP transport protocol, multiple SDP PDUs may be sent in a single L2CAP packet, but only one L2CAP packet per connection to a given SDP server may be outstanding at a given instant. Limiting SDP to sending one unacknowledged packet provides a simple form of flow control.

SDP—Service Attribute Definitions

Only service classes that directly support the SDP server are included in the SDP section of the Core. Additional service classes are defined in the Profiles section. It is likely that future revisions of the Bluetooth Specification will have additional service classes and modifications to these originals.

> **Service Discovery**
>
> As computing continues to move to a network-centric model, finding and making use of services that may be available in the network becomes increasingly important.
>
> Services can include common ones such as:
> - Printing
> - Paging
> - FAXing
>
> as well as various kinds of information access such as:
> - Teleconferencing
> - Network bridges
> - Access points
> - eCommerce facilities
>
> In addition, there are other resources such as:
>
> - Getting access to the services (finding and obtaining the protocols access methods, "drivers," and other code necessary to utilize the service)
> - Controlling access to the services
> - Advertising the services
> - Choosing among competing services, based on billing.

Chapter 4: Section-By-Section Summary

SDP—Background Information

The background information provides a good summary of the kinds of things one can do with an SDP, and the Bluetooth SDP in particular.

SDP—Example SDP Transactions

Addendum 2 of the SDP of the Spec has some example SDP transactions that are illustrative of SDP flows. The examples are not exhaustive and contain many simplifications.

> **Bluetooth Service Discovery**
>
> Bluetooth SDP addresses service discovery specifically for the Bluetooth environment. It is optimized for the highly dynamic nature of Bluetooth communications. SDP focuses primarily on discovering services available from or through Bluetooth devices. SDP does not define methods for accessing services; once services are discovered with SDP, they can be accessed in various ways, depending upon the service. This might include the use of other service discovery and access mechanisms.
>
> SDP provides a means for other Bluetooth high-level protocols to be used along with it, but it does not require them.

Chapter 4: Section-By-Section Summary

Communications Interfaces

In order to leverage the large number of communications-oriented applications that currently exist, Bluetooth wireless technology must interface to existing applications protocols and frameworks.

> **RFCOMM at a Glance**
> **Function**: Interfaces to standard communications protocols
>
> **Part**: F
>
> **Interfaces**: L2CAP, adopted upper layer protocols.

Section F of the Specification describes four of these adaptations as follows:

   1) RFCOMM with TS 07.10

   2) IrDA Interoperability

   3) Telephony Control Specification

   4) Interoperability requirements for Bluetooth communications as a Wireless Application Protocol (WAP) Bearer

All of these are cable replacement or, in the case of IrDA, cable-replacement-replacement technologies.

Communications Interfaces—RFCOMM with TS 07.10

RFCOMM is a serial communications protocol. Applications writers frequently use this protocol when designing a function that uses a serial communications

Chapter 4: Section-By-Section Summary

cable, especially one that works with a Global System for Mobile Communications (GSM) cell phone.

The RFCOMM protocol provides emulation of serial ports over the L2CAP protocol. The protocol is based on the ETSI GSM Technical Standard 07.10, version 6.3.0 (1997). The Bluetooth Specification does not encompass the complete Terminal Equipment to Mobile Station (TE-MS) multiplexer protocol standard, only the relevant parts for the emulation. Also, some adaptations of the TS 07.10 standard are specified.

RFCOMM emulates EIA/TIA-232 (ANSI/TIA/EIA-232-F-1997) serial ports with a built-in scheme for null modem emulation. The emulation also includes transfer of the state of non-data (voice) circuits. In most systems, RFCOMM will be part of a port driver that includes a serial port emulation entity.

The actual flow control between RFCOMM and the lower layer L2CAP is implementation dependent. RFCOMM has a virtual flow control mechanism that must be supported by the implementations that follow:

- Wired Serial Port Flow Control (RTS/CTS or XON/XOFF)
- RFCOMM Flow Control
- Port Emulation Entity Serial Flow Control

Chapter 4: Section-By-Section Summary

Unsupported TS 07.10 features in RFCOMM include the following:

- The Unnumbered Information (UI) command and response
- The error recovery mode option and the associated frame types
- The opening flag and the closing flags in the 07.10 basic option frame

The section on RFCOMM protocol concludes with two descriptions of how it should be used to emulate serial ports.

- Type 1 devices are communication endpoints such as computers and printers.
- Type 2 devices are part of a communication segment; e.g., modems.

Communications Interfaces—IrDA Interoperability

The Infrared OBject EXchange (IrOBEX, or OBEX for short) protocol has been adopted by the Bluetooth wireless technology. The Bluetooth implementation of OBEX offers the same features for applications as within the IrDA protocol hierarchy, enabling the applications to work

Chapter 4: Section-By-Section Summary

over either medium. It is a high-level protocol that deals, as the name implies, with data abstractions (objects).

The goal of the writers of this section of the Bluetooth Specification was to demonstrate that it is possible to develop application programs that function well over both short-range RF and IR media. The author posits that each media type has its advantages and disadvantages, but the goal for the sections is to show applications that work over both.

In an attempt to prevent fragmentation of the application domain, this section defines the intersection point where Bluetooth wireless technology and IrDA applications may converge. That intersection point is the IrDA IrOBEX (or OBEX).

The IrDA Interoperability section is dedicated to the model of OBEX objects and the OBEX session protocol. The section is to be read with the IrOBEX specification in hand, and is a good example of the leverage of existing protocols by the writers of the Bluetooth Specification.

The OBEX protocol can transfer an object by using the **Put** and **Get** operations. One object can be exchanged in one or more **Put** requests or **Get** responses. The model handles both information about the object (e.g., type) and the object itself.

Chapter 4: Section-By-Section Summary

There are two methods for implementing the OBEX protocol in the Bluetooth system. It may be implemented using the resources defined by RFCOMM or TCI/IP.

When OBEX is implemented using RFCOMM, certain criteria must be met. The Bluetooth devices supporting the OBEX protocol have to satisfy the following requirements:

> 1) The device supporting OBEX must be able to function as a client, a server, or both.
> 2) All servers running simultaneously on a device must use separate RFCOMM server channels.
> 3) Applications (service/server) using OBEX must be able to register the proper information into the service discovery database. This information for different application profiles is specified in the profile specifications.

OBEX is mapped over the TCP/IP to create reliable connection-oriented services. This section does not define how TCP/IP is mapped over Bluetooth wireless communications. The Bluetooth devices, which support the OBEX protocol over TCP/IP, must satisfy the following requirements:

> 1) The device supporting OBEX must be able to function as either a client, or a server, or both.

2) For the server, the TCP port number 650 is by Internet Assigned Number Authority (IANA). If an assigned number is not desirable, the port number can be a value above 1023. However, the use of the TCP port number (650) defined by IANA is highly recommended.

3) The client must use a port number (on the client side), which is not within the 0-1023 range.

4) Applications (service/server) using OBEX must be able to register the proper information into the service discovery database.

Bluetooth communications define three application profiles using OBEX. These profiles are:

1) Synchronization
2) File Transfer
3) Object Push

Communications Interfaces—Telephony Control Specification

The Bluetooth Telephony Control protocol Specification - Binary (TCS Binary), is a bit-oriented protocol. This protocol defines the call control signaling for establishing voice and data calls between Bluetooth devices. In addition, it defines mobility management procedures for handling Bluetooth TCS devices.

The TCS contains the following functionality:

- Call Control (CC)—signaling for the establishment and release of speech and data calls between Bluetooth devices
- Group Management—signaling to ease the handling of groups of Bluetooth devices
- ConnectionLess TCS (CL)—provisions to exchange signaling information not related to an ongoing call

Communications Interfaces—Interoperability requirements for Bluetooth as a WAP Bearer

The WAP is designed to provide Internet and Internet-like access to devices that are constrained in one or more ways. The WAP transport session protocols may be run over a number of cellular bearer services. This section notes that Bluetooth wireless technology may also be considered a bearer service, and defines the SDP records allowing the discovery of WAP servers with its facilities.

These include devices having limited:

- Communications bandwidth
- Memory
- Processing power
- Display capabilities
- Input devices

Chapter 4: Section-By-Section Summary

These factors fostered the development of WAP.

Many of the characteristics of Bluetooth devices are shared with the target platforms for the WAP. In some cases, the same device may be enabled for both types of communication. This section describes the interoperability requirements for using Bluetooth wireless technology with Point to Point Protocol (PPP) as the communications bearer for WAP protocols and applications.

The WAP environment typically consists of three types of devices:

1) WAP Client device
2) WAP Proxy/gateway
3) WAP Server

HCI

Early implementations of Bluetooth wireless technology will be executed using separately developed modules. The Host Controller Interface (HCI) specification tells precisely how this interface is supposed to work, both logically and physically.

> ### HCI at a Glance
> **Function**: Optional physical/logical interface if Bluetooth is embodied in a separate module
>
> **Part**: H
>
> **Interfaces**: L2CAP, LM, upper protocol

Chapter 4: Section-By-Section Summary

This section has four subsections of interest. They are as follows:

    1) Bluetooth HCI Functional Specification
    2) HCI USB Transport Layer
    3) HCI RS232 Transport Layer
    4) HCI UART Transport Layer

The first subsection is the logical view of the interface and the last three are the current examples of physical embodiments of HCI. Figure 9 shows where HCI fits in the Bluetooth protocol stack. The logical view explains the information flows, the Transport Layers document physical embodiments of interconnection.

HCI—Bluetooth Host Controller Interface Functional Specification

The HCI is the Bluetooth technology equivalent of the cable that connects a modem with a personal computer. Two essential classes of information travel across such an interface. The first is the payload information that would have traveled between a host and its communication system had they been in physical contact (integrated together). The second is the control and coordination information necessary to maintain the remote physical link. The HCI section covers both of these communications streams.

Chapter 4: Section-By-Section Summary

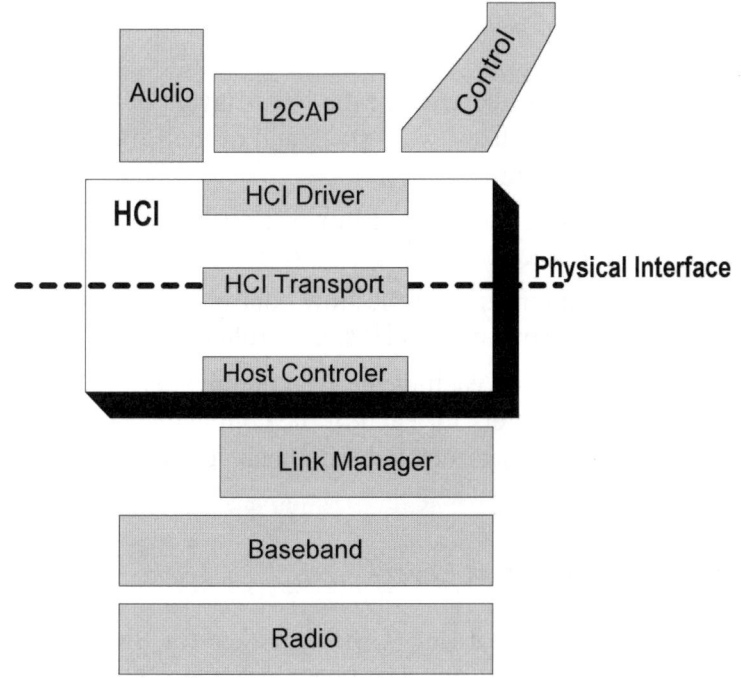

Figure 9—Block diagram

The first subsection of the HCI is required reading for anyone involved in interfacing or implementing a Bluetooth communications capability into a product. That much is obvious. What may not be obvious is that there are some signals and interfaces to the lower layers that are documented in the HCI section and are not defined anywhere else.

The HCI provides a uniform interface method of accessing the Bluetooth hardware capabilities. The Functional

Chapter 4: Section-By-Section Summary

Specification provides the following:

- A brief overview of the lower layers of the Bluetooth software stack and of the Bluetooth hardware
- An overview of the Lower HCI Device Driver Interface on the Host Device
- A description of the flow control used between the Host and the Host Controller
- Details of each of the HCI commands (parameters for each of the commands, and lists of events associated with each command)

HCI USB Transport Layer

The Universal Serial Bus (USB) interface for Bluetooth hardware is treated first. The text warns the readers that they should be familiar with USB, USB design issues, Advanced Configuration Power Interface (ACPI), the overall Bluetooth architecture, the basics of the radio interface, and with the Bluetooth Host Controller Interface in general.

HCI RS232 Transport Layer

The objective of the HCI RS232 Transport Layer is to make it possible to use the Bluetooth HCI over one physi-

Chapter 4: Section-By-Section Summary

cal RS232 interface between the Bluetooth Host and the Bluetooth Host Controller.

> **HCI IS IMPORTANT**
>
> Some aspects of the HCI have to do with the interface itself, but some of the commands described are necessary for the proper functioning of a Bluetooth unit, and are described here and nowhere else. If you need to understand the details of the Bluetooth protocols, it is very important to read and understand this first HCI section even if you don't intend to use or implement HCI!

HCI UART Transport Layer

The objective of the HCI Universal Asynchronous Receiver Transmitter (UART) Transport Layer is to make it possible to use the Bluetooth HCI over a serial interface between two UARTs on the same printed circuit board. The HCI UART Transport Layer assumes that the UART communication is free from line errors. This document describes the UART Transport Layer (between the Host and the Host Controller). HCI command, event, and data packets flow through this layer, but the layer does not decode them.

Chapter 4: Section-By-Section Summary

Testing

The test mode supports testing of the Bluetooth transmitter and receiver. It is intended mainly for certification/compliance testing of the

> *Testing at a Glance*
> **Function**: Attributes needed for certification and compliance testing
>
> **Part**: I
>
> **Interfaces**: Radio, Baseband, LMP, HCI

radio and Baseband layer, and may also be used for regulatory approval or in-production and after-sales testing. A device in test mode must not support normal operation.

The test mode is designed such that it allows no access to user data. This is done for security reasons, to ensure that someone cannot secretly turn on the test mode of your Bluetooth device and read your data, bypassing all security.

The topics covered in this section are as follows:

1. Bluetooth Test Mode
2. Compliance Requirements
3. Test Control Interface

Testing—Bluetooth Test Mode

Protocol testing will be used to verify the implemented functionality in the lowest layers for all Bluetooth accessory products, Bluetooth components, and Bluetooth products. This conformance testing is required to completely test the implementation.

The setup for testing consists of a device under test (DUT) and a tester (optionally, additional measurement equipment may be used). Tester and DUT form a piconet where the tester acts as master and has full control over the test procedure. The DUT acts as slave. The control is done via the air interface using LMP commands.

The test mode is a special state of the Bluetooth model. For security and type approval reasons, a device in test mode may not support "normal operation." In this state, no user data is able to be sent or received. The reason for this is to close a potential trap door access to secure communication. Without this safeguard, an eavesdropper could potentially go into test mode and pick off unauthorized information.

When the DUT leaves the test mode, it enters the standby state. After power-off, the Bluetooth device returns to standby state.

Testing—Compliance Requirements

The Bluetooth Promoters and the Bluetooth Adopters have signed agreements that grant them a Bluetooth license for products that comply with the Specification. This section documents the requirements that must be met. This must

Chapter 4: Section-By-Section Summary

be done for each product to be granted the rights extended by the Promoters' and Adopters' Agreements, respectively.

This section provides an overview of the requirements and the Bluetooth Qualification Program. The Bluetooth Qualification Program is the process by which a Promoter or an Adopter demonstrates that a particular product meets the requirements of the Specification. Regulatory requirements and governmental-type approval requirements are outside the scope of this section and the document in general.

Testing—Test Control Interface

In order to shield the tester from having to adapt to each and every implementation of Implementations Under Test (IUTs) or Systems Under Test (SUTs), the use of a standardized control interface has been mandated. It is described in this section. This mandate puts an extra burden upon the manufacturer of the IUT/SUT.

The manufacturer must do the following:

- Adopt the implementation-dependent interface to the TCI
- Supply, with the IUT, the adapter needed (can be hardware, software, or firmware)

Chapter 4: Section-By-Section Summary

The Bluetooth Test Control Interface (TCI) is used when verifying the Bluetooth protocol requirements for a Bluetooth accessory product, Bluetooth component, or a Bluetooth product. More specifically, the TCI will be used when verifying implemented functionality of the following:

- Baseband layer (the protocol-related part)
- Link Manager Protocol
- Logical Link Control and Adaptation Protocol
- Host Control Interface, if the manufacturer claims support of the HCI

Profiles

> *Profiles at a Glance*
> **Function**: Vertical slices of the Bluetooth protocol stack
>
> **Part**: K (second volume)
>
> **Interfaces**: all

Profiles have two essential features. They describe which Bluetooth protocols are to be used for a given application and how those specifications are to be used to ensure interoperability. They also describe other protocols outside the Bluetooth Specification or "user level" applications that are used to deliver interoperable applications.

For instance, the use of the PPP protocol or the Ir Mobile Communications (IrMC) data formats and applications are not discussed in the Core portion of the Bluetooth

Specification. The profiles freely use industry standards such as these. Therefore, not everything in the Profiles is taken out of the Core Specification.

Interoperability between devices from different manufacturers is provided for a specific service and use case, if the devices conform to a Bluetooth SIG-defined profile specification. A profile defines a selection of messages and procedures (generally termed *capabilities*) from the Bluetooth SIG specifications and gives an unambiguous description of the air interface for specified service(s) and use case(s). All defined features are process-mandatory. This means that, if a feature is used, it is used in a specified manner. Whether the provision of a feature is mandatory or optional is stated separately for both sides of the Bluetooth air interface.

The profiles defined are as follows:

1) Generic Access Profile

2) Service Discovery Profile Application Profile

3) Cordless Telephony Profile

4) Intercom Profile

5) Serial Port Profile

6) Headset Profile

7) Dial-up Networking Profile

8) Fax Profile

9) LAN Access Profile
10) Generic Object Exchange Profile
11) Object Push Profile
12) File Transfer Profile
13) Synchronization Profile

Generic Access Profile

The purpose of the Generic Access Profile is as follows:

- To introduce definitions, recommendations, and common requirements related to modes and access procedures that are to be used by transport and application profiles.

- To describe how devices are to behave in standby and connecting states in order to guarantee that links and channels can always be established between Bluetooth devices, and that multi-profile operation is possible. Special focus is put on discovery, link establishment, and security procedures.

- To state requirements on user interface aspects, mainly coding schemes and names of procedures and parameters, which are needed to guarantee a satisfactory user experience.

Chapter 4: Section-By-Section Summary

Service Discovery Profile Application Profile

The service discovery profile defines the protocols and procedures that are used by a service discovery application on a device to locate services in other Bluetooth devices. It utilizes the Bluetooth Service Discovery Protocol (SDP).

The service discovery application in this profile is a specific user-initiated application. This profile contrasts with other profiles where service discovery interactions between two SDP entities in two Bluetooth devices result from the need to enable a particular transport service (e.g., RFCOMM), or a particular usage scenario (e.g., file transfer, cordless telephony, LAN AP) over these two devices.

Cordless Telephony Profile

This profile defines the features and procedures that are required for interoperability between different units active in the "3-in-1 phone" use case. The "3-in-1 phone" is a solution for providing an extra mode of operation to cellular phones, using Bluetooth wireless technology as a short-range bearer for accessing fixed network telephony services via a base station. The scope of this profile includes the following layers, protocols, and profiles:

Chapter 4: Section-By-Section Summary

- Bluetooth Baseband
- Link Manager Protocol
- L2CAP
- Service Discovery Protocol
- Telephony Control Protocol Specification (TCS-Binary)
- General Access Profile

The "3-in-1 phone" use case can also be applied generally for wireless telephony in a residential or small office environment, for example, for cordless-only telephony or cordless telephony services in a PC.

Intercom Profile

The Intercom profile defines the protocols and procedures that are used by devices implementing the intercom part of the usage model called "3-in-1 phone." This is often referred to as the "walkie-talkie" usage of Bluetooth wireless technology.

Serial Port Profile

This profile defines the requirements for Bluetooth devices to set up emulated serial cable connections using RFCOMM between two peer devices. The Serial Port profile defines the protocols and procedures that are used by devices using Bluetooth wireless communications for RS232 (or similar) serial cable emulation. The scenario covered by this profile supports legacy applications using Bluetooth wireless communications as a cable replacement through a virtual serial port abstraction.

Headset Profile

The Headset profile defines the protocols and procedures that are used by devices implementing the usage model called "Ultimate Headset." The most common examples of such devices are audio system headsets, personal computer sound systems, and cellular phones. The headset can be wirelessly connected for the purposes of acting as the device's audio input and output mechanism, providing full duplex audio. The headset increases the user's mobility while maintaining call privacy.

Dial-up Networking Profile

The Dial-up Networking profile defines the protocols and procedures that are used by devices implementing the usage model called "Internet Bridge." The most common examples of such devices are modems and cellular phones.

The scenarios covered by this profile include the following:

- Use of a cellular phone or modem by a computer as a wireless modem for connecting to a dial-up Internet access server, or using other dial-up services

- Use of a cellular phone or modem by a computer to receive data calls

Fax Profile

The Fax profile defines the protocols and procedures that are used by devices implementing the fax part of the usage model called "Data Access Points, Wide Area Networks." A Bluetooth cellular phone or modem may be located by a computer as a wireless fax modem to send or receive a fax message.

LAN Access Profile

This document is a LAN Access profile for Bluetooth devices. It defines how Bluetooth devices can access the services of a LAN using PPP. It also shows how the same PPP mechanisms are used to form a network consisting of two Bluetooth devices. This profile defines LAN Access as using PPP over RFCOMM.

The profile mentions that PPP is capable of supporting various networking protocols (e.g., IP, IPX) but does not mandate the use of any particular protocol.

Chapter 4: Section-By-Section Summary

The profile defines how PPP networking is supported in the following situations:

1) LAN Access for a single Bluetooth device
2) LAN Access for multiple Bluetooth devices
3) PC to PC (using PPP networking over serial cable emulation)

Generic Object Exchange Profile

The Generic Object Exchange profile (GOEP) defines the protocols and procedures that are used by the applications providing the usage models that need the object exchange capabilities. The usage model can be, for example, Synchronization, File Transfer, or Object Push model. The most common devices using these usage models can be:

- Notebook PCs
- Personal digital assistants (PDAs)
- Smart phones
- Mobile phones

Object Push Profile

The Object Push profile defines the requirements for the protocols and procedures that are used by the applications providing the Object Push usage model. This profile makes use of the GOEP to define the interoperability requirements for the protocols needed by applications. The most common devices using these usage models can be notebook PCs, PDAs, and mobile phones.

The scenarios covered by this profile include the following uses of a Bluetooth device:

- A mobile phone to push an object to the inbox of another Bluetooth device. The object can, for example, be a business card or an appointment.
- A mobile phone to pull a business card from another Bluetooth device.
- A mobile phone to exchange business cards with another Bluetooth device. Exchange is defined as a push of a business card followed by a pull of a business card.

File Transfer Profile

This application profile defines the application requirements for Bluetooth devices necessary for the support of the File Transfer usage model. The requirements are expressed in terms of end-user services and by defining the features and procedures that are required for interoperability between Bluetooth devices in the File Transfer usage model. The File Transfer profile defines the requirements for the protocols and procedures that are used by the applications providing the File Transfer usage model. This profile uses the GOEP as a base profile to define the interoperability requirements for the protocols needed by the applications. The most common devices using these usage models can be, but are not limited to, personal computers, notebook computers, and PDAs.

The scenarios covered by this profile are the following:

- Use of a Bluetooth device, such as a notebook PC, to browse an object store (file system) of another Bluetooth device. Browsing involves viewing objects (files and folders) and navigating the folder hierarchy of another Bluetooth device.
- Transfer of objects (files and folders) between two Bluetooth devices. For example, copying files from one PC to another PC.
- Manipulation of objects (files and folders) on another Bluetooth device. This includes deleting objects, and creating new folders.

Synchronization Profile

The Synchronization profile defines the requirements for the protocols and procedures that are used by the applications providing the Synchronization usage model. This profile makes use of the GOEP to define the interoperability requirements for the protocols needed by applications.

Chapter 4: Section-By-Section Summary

The most common devices using these usage models might be personal computers, notebook computers, PDAs, and mobile phones.

The scenarios covered by this profile are as follows:

- Use of a mobile phone or PDA by a computer to exchange Personal Information Management (PIM) data, including necessary log information to ensure that the data contained within their respective Object Stores is made identical. Examples of the PIM data are phonebook and calendar items.

- Initiation of the previous scenario (Sync Command Feature).

- Automatic start of synchronization when a mobile phone or PDA enters the RF proximity of the computer.

Appendices

Appendix I is one of the eleven places where Acronyms and/or Abbreviations are listed in the Specification. This decentralized approach is the reason this Guide has a *Consolidated Glossary* (see Chapter 5).

> *Appendices at a Glance*
> **Function**: Late additions and miscellaneous options and addendums
>
> **Part**: Appendices to the Core
>
> **Interfaces**: Various

Chapter 4: Section-By-Section Summary

If you are implementing Encryption, you will need the information in Appendix II, Encryption Sample Data. If not, it won't be very interesting.

Appendix III presents Bluetooth Audio. This Appendix offers recommendations and general guidelines for voice transmission over the Bluetooth air interface. The recommendation is formed so that a smooth audio interface of a Bluetooth terminal to other audio, electronic devices, and cellular terminal equipment can be carried out. It makes recommendations for the following:

- Maximum sound pressure
- Other telephony network requirements
- Audio levels for Bluetooth
- Microphone path
- Loudspeaker path
- Bluetooth voice interface
- Frequency mask

The Baseband Timers (Appendix IV) contains the definitions of all the timers defined in the Baseband section. They are as follows:

- inquiryTO
- pageTO
- pagerespTO

Chapter 4: Section-By-Section Summary

- inqrespTO
- newconnectionTO
- supervisionTO

In theory, several paging schemes may be used for the access procedures. In fact, currently there is one mandatory paging scheme that has to be supported by all Bluetooth devices and one optional one. Appendix V documents this optional scheme.

The main difference between the optional paging scheme and the mandatory scheme is the construction of the page train sent by the pager. In addition to transmission in the even master slots, the master transmits in the odd master slots as well. This allows the slave unit to reduce its scan window.

Appendix VI, Bluetooth Assigned Numbers, is a good reference for those who need the detailed data presented here, but it is not for the general reader.

Appendix VII, Message Sequence Chart between Host - Host Controller/Link Manager, is a very important tutorial. Many behaviors and origins of behaviors of the LM are explained here. It shows examples of interworking between HCI Commands and LM Protocol Data Units in the form of MSCs. It not only helps to understand and correctly use the HCI Commands, it presents much of the management functions that are not explicitly called out in the rest of the Specification.

Consolidated Glossary

> **Chapter 5**
> Glossary

Many (but not all) parts of the Bluetooth Specification have their own set of acronym listings and/or glossary. The names, placement, and format of these definitions are not consistent throughout the document. In a few cases, acronyms or definitions are different in different sections. This chapter provides a comprehensive listing of all the acronyms and terms defined for Bluetooth technology.

The generalized format for the listings is as follows:

| Term | {1.} definition or explanation [where defined] {[where]} {2.} second definition [where defined] |

where the items in braces exist only if there are multiple definitions for the term. The codes for the sections where definitions reside are as follows:

CODE	Location
L2CAP	Part D, Logical Link Control Protocol
RFCOMM	Part F1, RFCOMM with TS 07.10
IrDA	Part F2, IrDA Interoperability
HCI	Part H1, Host Controller Interface
TCI	Part I3, Test Control Interface
AN	Appendix IIIV, Bluetooth Assigned numbers
MSCs	Appendix IX, Message Sequence Charts
Profiles	Profiles Appendix III
Core	Core Appendix III
GAP	Part K1, Generic Access Profile
SDAP	Part K2, Service Discovery Application Profile

Chapter 5: Consolidated Glossary

A

ACK	Acknowledge [Core]
ACL	Asynchronous Connection Less [HCI]
ACL	Asynchronous Connectionless [Profiles]
ACL link	Asynchronous Connection-Less link. Provides a packet-switched connection. (Master to any slave). [Core]
ACL link	An asynchronous (packet-switched) connection 1 between two devices created on LMP level. Traffic on an ACL link uses ACL packets to be transmitted. [GAP]
ACO	Authenticated Ciphering Offset [Core]
AG	Audio Gateway [Profiles]
AM_ADDR	Active Member Address [Core]
AP	Access Point [Profiles]
AR_ADDR	Access Request Address [Core]
ARQ	Automatic Repeat reQuest [Core]
Authenticated Device	A Bluetooth device, whose identity has been verified during the lifetime of the current link, based on the authentication procedure. [GAP]
Authentication	A generic procedure based on LMP-authentication if a link key exists or on LMP-pairing if no link key exists. [GAP]
Authorization	A procedure where a user of a Bluetooth device grants a specific (remote) Bluetooth device access to a specific service. Authorization implies that the identity of the remote device can be verified through authentication. [GAP]

Chapter 5: Consolidated Glossary

Authorize	The act of granting a specific Bluetooth device access to a specific service. It may be based upon user confirmation, or given the existence of a trusted relationship. [GAP]

B

Baseband	The Bluetooth baseband specifies the medium access and physical layers procedures to support the exchange of real-time voice and data information streams and ad-hoc net working between Bluetooth units. [Core] [L2CAP] [AN]
BB	BaseBand (see LC) [TCI] [Profiles] [Core]
BCH	Bose, Chaudhuri & Hocquenghem. Type of code. The persons who discovered these codes in 1959 (H) and 1960 (B&C). [Core]
BD_ADDR	Bluetooth Device Address [HCI] [Profiles] [Core]
BER	Bit Error Rate [Core]
Bluetooth	Bluetooth is a wireless communication link, operating in the unlicensed ISM band at 2,4 GHz using a frequency hopping tranceiver. It allows real-time voice and data communications between Bluetooth Hosts. The link protocol is based on time slots. [Core]

Chapter 5: Consolidated Glossary

Bluetooth Host	Bluetooth Host is a computing device, peripheral, cellular telephone, access point to PSTN network, etc. A Bluetooth Host attached to a Bluetooth unit may communicate with other Bluetooth Hosts attached to their Bluetooth units as well. The communication channel through the Bluetooth units provides almost wire-like transparency. [Core]
Bluetooth Unit	Bluetooth Unit is a voice/data circuit equipment for a short-range wireless communication link. It allows voice and data communications between Bluetooth Hosts. [Core]
Bond	A relation between two Bluetooth devices defined by creating, exchanging and storing a common link key. The bond is created through the bonding or LMP-pairing procedures. [GAP]
Bonding	A dedicated procedure for performing the first authentication, where a common link key is created and stored for future use. [GAP]
BT	Bandwidth Time [Core]

C

CAC	Channel Access Code [Core]
CC	Call Control [Core] [Profiles]
Channel	A logical connection on L2CAP level between two devices serving a single application or higher layer protocol. [GAP]

Chapter 5: Consolidated Glossary

Channel establishment	A procedure for establishing a channel on L2CAP level. [GAP]
CL	Connectionless [Profiles] [Profiles]
CO	Connection-oriented
CoD	Class Of Device [Profiles]
CODEC	Coder DECoder [Core]
COF	Ciphering Offset [Core]
Connect (to service)	The establishment of a connection to a service. If not already done, this includes establishment of a physical link, link and channel as well. [GAP]
Connectable device	A Bluetooth device in range that will respond to a page. [GAP]
Connecting	A phase in the communication between devices when a connection between them is being established. (Connecting phase follows after the link establishment phase is completed.) [GAP]
Connection	A connection between two peer applications or higher layer protocols mapped onto a channel. [GAP]
Connection-establishment	A procedure for creating a connection mapped onto a channel. [GAP]
Conscious	(usually referred to) a process that requires the explicit intervention of a user to be accomplished [SDAP]

Chapter 5: Consolidated Glossary

Coverage area	The area where two Bluetooth units can exchange messages with acceptable quality and performance. [Core]
CRC	Cyclic Redundancy Check [Core]
Creation of a secure connection	A procedure of establishing a connection, including authentication and encryption. [GAP]
Creation of a trusted relationship	A procedure where the remote device is marked as a trusted device. This includes storing a common link key for future authentication and pairing (if the link key is not available). [GAP]
CTP	Cordless Telephony Profile [Profiles]
CVSD	Continuous Variable Slope Delta Modulation [Core]

D

DAC	Device Access Code [Profiles] [Core]
DCE	1. Data Communication Equipment [Core] 2. Data Circuit-Terminating Equipment In serial communications, DCE refers to a device between the communication endpoints whose sole task is to facilitate the communications process; typically a modem [RFCOMM] [Core]
DCI	Default Check Initialization [Core]
Device discovery	A procedure for retrieving the Bluetooth device address, clock, class-of-device field and used page scan mode from discoverable devices. [GAP]

Chapter 5: Consolidated Glossary

DH	Data-High Rate. Data packet type for high rate data. [Core] [HCI]
DIAC	Dedicated Inquiry Access Code [HCI][Profiles] [Core]
Discoverable device	A Bluetooth device in range that will respond to an inquiry (normally in addition to responding to page). [GAP]
DM	Data - Medium Rate. Data packet type for medium rate data. [Core] [HCI]
DT	Data Terminal [Profiles]
DTE	Data Terminal Equipment in serial communications, DTE refers to a device at the endpoint of the communications path; typically a computer or terminal [RFCOMM] [Core]
DTMF	Dual Tone Multiple Frequency [Core]
DUT	Device Under Test [HCI] [Core]
DV	Data Voice Data. Packet type for data and voice. [Core] [HCI]

E

ETSI	European Telecommunications Standards Institute [Core]

F

FCC	Federal Communications Commission [Core]
FEC	Forward Error Correction code [Core]

Chapter 5: Consolidated Glossary

FH	Frequency Hopping [Core]
FHS	Frequency Hopping Synchronization [Profiles] [Core]
FIFO	First In First Out [Core]
FSK	Frequency Shift Keying type of modulation [Core]
FW	Firmware [TCI] [Core]

G

GAP	Generic Access Profile [Profiles]
GEOP	Generic Object Exchange Profile [IrDA] [Core]
GFSK	Gaussian Frequency Shift Keying [Core]
GIAC	General Inquiry Access Code [HCI] [Profiles] [Core]
GM	Group Management [Profiles] [Core]
GOEP	Generic Object Exchange Profile [Profiles]
GW	Gateway [Profiles]

H

HA	Host Application SW using Bluetooth [Core]
HC	1. Host Controller [MSCs] 2. Host Controller Interface [Core]
HCI	Host Controller Interface [HCI] [TCI] [MSCs] [Profiles]
HEC	Header-Error-Check [Core]

Chapter 5: Consolidated Glossary

HID	Human Interface Device [Core]
Host Terminal interface	Host terminal interface is the Interface between Bluetooth Host and Bluetooth Unit. [Core]
HS	Headset [Profiles]
HV	High quality Voice; e.g., HV1 packet [Core]
HW	Hardware [TCI] [Core]

I

IAC	Inquiry Access Code [Core]
Idle	As seen from a remote device, a Bluetooth device is idle, or is in idle mode, when there is no link established between them. [GAP]
IEEE	Institute of Electrical and Electronics Engineerings, Inc. [Core]
IETF	Internet Engineering Task Force [L2CAP] [AN] [Core]
Inquiry	A Bluetooth unit transmits inquiry messages in order to discover the other Bluetooth units that are active within the coverage area. The Bluetooth units that capture inquiry messages may send a response to the inquiring Bluetooth unit. The response contains information about the Bluetooth unit itself and its Bluetooth Host. [Core]
IP	Internet Protocol [L2CAP] [AN] [Profiles] [Core]
IPX	Internet Protocol eXchange [Profiles]

Chapter 5: Consolidated Glossary

IrDA	Infra-red Data Association [L2CAP] [IrDA] [AN] [Profiles] [Core]
IrMC	Ir Mobile Communications [IrDA] [Profiles] [Core]
ISDN	Integrated Services Digital Net-works [Core]
ISM	Industrial, Scientific, Medical [Core]
Isochronous user channel	Channel used for time bounded information like i.e., compressed audio (ACL link). [Core]
IUT	Implementation Under Test [TCI] [Core]

K

Known	(with respect to a specific device) opposite to unknown; a known devices is not necessarily a paired device [SDAP]
Known device	A Bluetooth device for which at least the BD_ADDR is stored. [GAP]

L

L_CH	Logical Channel [L2CAP] [HCI] [Core]
L2CA	1. Logical Link Control and Adaption. Logical Link Control And Management part of the Bluetooth protocol stack. [Core] [TCI] [Profiles] 2. Logical Link Control and Adaptation, protocol multiplexer layer for Bluetooth [AN]

Chapter 5: Consolidated Glossary

L2CAP	Logical Link Control and Adaptation Protocol [HCI] [IrDA] [TCI] [Profiles] [Core]
LAN	Local Area Network [Profiles]
LAP	1. Lower Address Part [HCI] [MSCs] [Core] 2. LAN Access Point [Profiles]
LC	1. Link Controller (or baseband) part of the Bluetooth protocol stack [TCI] 2. Link Controller (or baseband) part of the Bluetooth protocol stack. Low level Baseband protocol handler. [Core] 3. Link Controller [L2CAP] [HCI] [MSCs] [Profiles]
LCP	Link Control Protocol [TCI] [Core]
LCSS	Link Controller Service Signaling [Core]
LFSR	Linear Feedback Shift Register [Core]
LIAC	Limited Inquiry Access Code [Profiles]
Link	Shorthand for an ACL link. [GAP]
Link establishment	A procedure for establishing a link on LMP level. A link is established when both devices have agreed that LMP setup is completed. [GAP]
LM	Link Manager [L2CAP] [HCI] [TCI] [MSCs] [Profiles] [Core]
LMP	1. Link Manager Protocol [L2CAP] [HCI] [TCI] [AN] [MSCs] [Profiles] 2. Link Manager Protocol. For LM peer-to-peer communication. [Core]

Chapter 5: Consolidated Glossary

LMP-authentication	An LMP level procedure for verifying the identity of a remote device. The procedure is based on a challenge-response mechanism using a random number, a secret key and the BD_ADDR of the non-initiating device. The secret key used can be a previously exchanged link key or an initialization key created based on a PIN (as used when pairing). [GAP]
LMP-pairing	A procedure that authenticates two devices, based on a PIN, and subsequently creates a common link key that can be used as a basis for a trusted relationship or a (single) secure connection. The procedure consists of the steps: creation of an initialization key (based on a random number and a PIN), LMP-authentication based on the initialization key and creation of a common link key. [GAP]
LocDev	Local Device [Profiles]
Logical Channel	The different types of channels on a Physical Link. [Core]
LSB	1. Least Significant Byte [IrDA] 2. Least Significant Bit [Core]

M

M	Master or Mandatory (Core)
M_ADDR	Medium Access Control Address [Core]
MAC 1	Medium Access Control Address [Core]
MAPI	Messaging Application Procedure Interface [Core]

Chapter 5: Consolidated Glossary

ME	Management Entity [Profiles]
MM	Mobility Management [Profiles]
MMI	Man-Machine Interface [TCI] [Core]
Mode	A set of directives that defines how a device will respond to certain events. [GAP]
MS	1. Mobile Station [Core] 2. Multiplexing sublayer (Core)
MSB	1. Most Significant Byte [IrDA] 2. Most Significant Bit
MSC	Message Sequence Chart [MSCs] [Profiles] [Core]
MTU	Maximum Transmission Unit [L2CAP] [AN] [Profiles] [Core]
MUX	Multiplexing Sublayer. A sublayer of the L2CAP layer. [Core]

N

NAK	Negative Acknowledge [Core]
Name discovery	A procedure for retrieving the user-friendly name (the Bluetooth device name) of a connectable device. [GAP]
NAP	Non-significant Address Part [Core]
new	(RemDev) (with regard to this profile) an additional remote device (RemDev) that is discovered during a Bluetooth inquiry, and that is not already connected to local device (LocDev) [SDAP]

Chapter 5: Consolidated Glossary

O

O	Optional [Core]
OBEX	Object Exchange Protocol [IrDA] [Profiles] [Core]
OCF	Opcode Command Field [HCI] [TCI] [Core]
OGR	OpCode Group Field [HCI]

P

Packet	Format of aggregated bits that can be transmitted in 1, 3, or 5 time slots. [Core]
PAGE	A baseband state where a device transmits page trains, and processes any eventual responses to the page trains. [GAP]
Page	The transmission by a device of page trains containing the Device Access Code of the device to which the physical link is requested. [GAP]
PAGE_SCAN	A baseband state where a device listens for page trains. [GAP]
Page scan	The listening by a device for page trains containing its own Device Access Code. [GAP]
Paging	1. A Bluetooth unit transmits paging messages in order to set up a communication link to another Bluetooth unit who is active within the coverage area. [Core]. 2. A procedure for establishing a physical link of ACL type on Baseband level, consisting of a page action of the initiator and a page scan action of the responding device. [GAP]

Chapter 5: Consolidated Glossary

Paired device	A Bluetooth device with which a link key has been exchanged (either before connection establishment was requested or during connecting phase). [GAP]
PC	Personal Computer [Profiles]
PCM	Pulse Coded Modulation [Core]
PCMCIA	Personal Computer Memory Card International Association [Core]
PDA	Personal Digital Assistant [Profiles]
PDU	Protocol Data Unit [IrDA] [MSCs] [Profiles] [Core]
Physical Channel	1. Synchronized RF hopping sequence in a piconet [Core] 2. A synchronized Bluetooth baseband-compliant RF hopping sequence. [GAP]
Physical Link	1. Connection between devices. [Core] 2. A Baseband-level connection {The term *connection* used here is not identical to the definition below. It is used in the absence of a more concise term.} between two devices established using paging. A physical link comprises a sequence of transmission slots on a physical channel alternating between master and slave transmission slots. [GAP]

Chapter 5: Consolidated Glossary

Piconet	1. In the Bluetooth system, the channel is shared among several Bluetooth units. The units sharing a common channel constitute a piconet. [Core] 2. A set of Bluetooth devices sharing the same physical channel defined by the master parameters (clock and BD_ADDR). [GAP]
PIM	Personal Information Management [Profiles]
PIN	Personal Identification Number [Core]
PM_ADDR	Parked Member Address [Core]
PN	Pseudo-random Noise [Core]
PnP	Plug and Play [AN] [Core]
POTS	Plain Old Telephone system [Core]
PPM	Part Per Million [Core]
PPP	Point-to-Point Protocol [L2CAP] [AN] [Profiles] [Core]
PRBS	Pseudo Random Bit Sequence [Core]
Pre-paired device	A Bluetooth device with which a link key was exchanged, and the link key is stored, before link establishment. [GAP]
Private	A mode of operation whereby a device can only be found via Bluetooth baseband pages; i.e. it only enters page scans [SDAP]
PRNG	Pseudo Random Noise Generation [Core]
PSTN	Public Switched Telephone Network [Profiles] [Core]

Chapter 5: Consolidated Glossary

Public	A mode of operation whereby a device can be found via Bluetooth baseband inquiries; i.e. it enters into inquiry scans. A public device also enters into page scans (contrast this with private) [SDAP]

Q

QoS	Quality Of Service [Profiles] [Core]

R

RAND	Random number [Core]
Reliable	Characteristic of an L2CAP channel that has an infinite flush timeout [L2CAP]
RemDev	Remote Device [Profiles]
RF	1. Radio Frequency [HCI] [Core] 2. Radio part of the Bluetooth protocol stack [TCI]
RFC	Request For Comments [L2CAP] [AN] [Core]
RFCOMM	1. Serial cable emulation protocol based on ETSI TS 07.10 [IrDA] [Core] 2. Serial Cable Emulation Protocol [Profiles]
RFCOMM Client	An RFCOMM client is an application that requests a connection to another application (RFCOMM server) [RFCOMM] [Core]
RFCOMM initiator	The device initiating the RFCOMM session; i.e. setting up RFCOMM channel on L2CAP and starting RFCOMM multiplexing with the SABM command frame on DLCI 0 (zero) [RFCOMM] [Core]

Chapter 5: Consolidated Glossary

RFCOMM Server	An RFCOMM server is an application that awaits a connection from an RFCOMM client on another device. What happens after such a connection is established is out of scope of this definition. [Core]
RFCOMM Server Channel	This is a subfield of the TS 07.10 DLCI number. This abstraction is used to allow both server and client applications to reside on both sides of an RFCOMM session. [RFCOMM] [Core]
RSSI	Received Signal Strength Indication [HCI] [Core]
RX	Receiver [Core]

S

S	Slave [Core]
SAP	Service Access Points [AN] [Core]
SAR	Segmentation and Reassembly [L2CAP] [AN] [Core]
Scatternet	Two or more piconets co-located in the same area (with or without inter-piconet communication). [Core]
SCO	Synchronous Connection Oriented [HCI]

Chapter 5: Consolidated Glossary

SCO link	1. A synchronous (circuit-switched) connection {The term *connection* used here is not identical to the definition below. It is used in the absence of a more concise term.} for reserved band width communications; e.g. voice between two devices, created on the LMP level by reserving slots periodically on a physical channel. Traffic on an SCO link uses SCO packets to be transmitted. SCO links can be established only after an ACL link has first been established. [GAP] 2. Synchronous Connection-Oriented link. Supports time-bounded information like voice. (Master to single slave) [Core]
SD	Service Discovery [IrDA] [Profiles] [Core]
SDDB	Service Discovery Database [IrDA] [Profiles] [Core]
SDP	Service Discovery Protocol [IrDA] [Profiles] [Core]
SeP	Serial Port [Profiles]
SEQN	Sequential Numbering scheme [Core]
Service Discovery	1. The ability to discover the capability of connecting devices or hosts. [AN] [Core] 2. Procedures for querying and browsing for services offered by or through another Bluetooth device. [GAP]
SIG	Special Interest Group [Profiles]

Chapter 5: Consolidated Glossary

Silent device	A Bluetooth device appears as silent to a remote device if it does not respond to inquiries made by the remote device. A device may be silent due to being non-discoverable or due to baseband congestion while being discoverable. [GAP]
SRES	Signed Response [Core]
SrvDscApp	Service Discovery Application [Profiles]
SS	Supplementary Services [Core]
SSI	Signal Strength Indication [Core]
SUT	System Under Test [TCI] [Core]
SW	Software [TCI] [Core]

T

TAE	Terminal Adapter Equipment [Core]
TBD	To Be Defined [HCI] [Core]
TC	Test Control layer for the test interface [TCI] [Core]
TCI	Test Control Interface [TCI] [Core]
TCP	Transport Control Protocol [Profiles]
TCP/IP	Transport Control Protocol/Internet Protocol [IrDA] [Core]
TCS	1. Telephony Control Specification [Profiles] 2. Telephony Control protocol Specification [Core]
TDD	Time-Division Duplex [Core]

Chapter 5: Consolidated Glossary

Time Slot	The Physical Channel is divided into 625 µs long time slots. [Core]
TL	Terminal [Profiles]
TLO	Terminal Originating A Call [Profiles]
TLT	Terminal Terminating A Call [Profiles]
Trusted device	A paired device that is explicitly marked as trusted. [GAP]
Trusting	The marking of a paired device as trusted. Trust marking can be done by the user, or automatically by the device (e.g., when in pairable mode) after asuccessful pairing. [GAP]
TTP	Tiny Transport Protocol. Between OBEX and UDP [TBD] [Core]
TX	Transmit [Core]

U

UA	User Asynchronous. Asynchronous user data [HCI] [Core]
UAP	Upper Address Part [Core]
UART	Universal Asynchronous receiver Transmitter [TCI] [Core]
UC	User Control [Core]
UDP	User Datagram Protocol [Profiles]
UDP/IP	User Datagram Protocol/Internet Protocol [Core]

Chapter 5: Consolidated Glossary

UI	1. User Interface [Profiles] 2. User Isochronous. Isochronous user data. [HCI] [Core]
UIAC	Unlimited Inquiry Access Code [Profiles] [Core]
Unconscious	Opposite to conscious (a process that requires the explicit intervention of a user to be accomplished) [SDAP]
Unknown	(with respect to a specific device) any other device that a specific device has no record of [SDAP]
Un-known device	A Bluetooth device for which no information (BD_ADDR, link key or other) is stored. [GAP]
Un-paired device	A Bluetooth device for which there was no exchanged link key available before connection establishment was request. [GAP]
US	User Synchronous. Synchronous user data. [HCI] [Core]
USB	Universal Serial Bus [HCI] [TCI] [Core]
UT	Upper Tester [TCI] [Core]
UUID	Universally Unique Identifier [Profiles]

W

WAP	Wireless Application Protocol [Core]
WUG	Wireless User Group [Profiles] [Core]

Bluetooth Special Interest Group

Bluetooth wireless technology is a specification for small form factor, low-cost, wireless communication and networking between PCs, mobile phones, and other portable devices. The Bluetooth Special Interest Group (SIG) is driven by the common goal of revolutionizing connectivity for both personal and business mobile devices. The initial "Promoter" group formed the SIG in May of 1998. The companies were:

> ### Chapter 6
> - Bluetooth Special Interest Group
> - Bluetooth Documents
> - References

- Ericsson
- IBM Corporation
- Intel Corporation
- Nokia
- Toshiba Corporation

In 1999, the SIG expanded to a nine-company Promoter group by adding:

- 3Com Corporation
- Lucent Technologies
- Microsoft Corporation
- Motorola Inc.

Chapter 6: Further Resources

The SIG membership has grown to over 2,000 members. The Promoter group companies are combining their respective skills to help drive the program forward as Bluetooth enabled products come to market.

At least two classes of membership other than Promoter currently exist. They are Early Adopters and Associates. Becoming a Bluetooth SIG member basically means that you sign a no-cost license agreement giving you the right to use the Specification for developing and manufacturing products and software using the Bluetooth Specification.

Early Adopter members are allowed to become involved with the SIG by participating in certain key meetings as well as having early access to working drafts of specifications for new Bluetooth functions.

Associate members have additional privileges over the Early Adopters. They can increase their level of involvement in the Bluetooth SIG by gaining earlier access to working drafts of specifications for new Bluetooth functions by becoming active in technical working groups. Also, they have the promotional benefits associated with being a high-profile member of the Bluetooth SIG.. Bluetooth Associate membership requires the sponsorship of a SIG Promoter Company.

Bluetooth Documents

The Bluetooth SIG's documents are available on their website at http://www.bluetooth.com/. Note that you must be a member of the SIG to get some of the documents. The vast majority of the documents are in Adobe Acrobat™ format (PDF). The free PDF reader is available at http://www.adobe.com/products/acrobat/readstep.html.

Further Resources

[1] Comer, Douglas E., <u>Internetworking With TCP/IP: Principles, Protocols, and Architecture</u>. Englewood Cliffs, NJ: Prentice Hall, 1988.

[2] Golio, Michael, Ed., <u>Modern Microwave and RF Handbook</u>. Boca Raton, FL: CRC Press, to be published 2000.

[3] International Standards Organization [July 1986b], Information Processing Systems—Open Systems Interconnection—Transport Service Definition, International Standard number 8072, ISO, Switzerland.

[4] Meehan, Aidan, <u>Celtic Design: The Dragon and The Griffin, The Viking Impact</u>. New York: Thames and Hudson, 1995.

[5] Miller, Brent A., Bisdikian, Chatschik, <u>Bluetooth Revealed</u>. Upper Saddle River, NJ: Prentice-Hall, 2001.
[5] Muller, Nathan J., <u>Bluetooth Demystified</u>. New York: McGraw-Hill, 2001.

[6] Naugle, Matthew G., <u>Network Protocol Handbook</u>. New York: McGraw-Hill, 1994.

[7] O'Hara, Bob, Petrick, Al, <u>IEEE 802.11 Handbook: A Designer's Companion</u>. New York: Standards Information Network, IEEE Press, 1999.

Index

Numerals

3-in-1 phone application, 32

A

ACK, 112
ACL (Asynchronous Connectionless) links, 48-49, 72, 112
ACO, 112
Addressing, 59-60
AG, 112
Airplane environment, 25-26
AM_ADDR, 112
AP, 112
Application examples, 31-35
AR_ADDR, 112
ARQ, 112
Asynchronous Connectionless (ACL) links, 48-49, 72, 112
Audio, 58-59, 97-98
Authenticated Device, 112
Authentication procedure, 65, 112
Authorization, 112
Authorize, 113
AUX1 packets, 72

B

Baseband, 43, 113
Baseband part of specification
    Audio Interface, 58-59
    Channel Control, 55-56
    Data Whitening, 53
    Device Addressing, 59-60
    Error Correction, 51-52
    General Description, 45-47
    Hop Selection, 56-58
    Logical Channels, 52-53
    Packet Formats, 49

Index

    Physical Channel, 46, 48
    Physical Link, 48-49
    Security, 60-62
    Transmit/Receive Routines, 54
    Transmit/Receive Timing, 54-55
Baseband Timers appendix, 108
Basic concepts, 7
BB, 113
BCH, 113
BD_ADDR, 59, 113
BER, 113
Blätand, Harald, 9
Bluetooth (the man), 9
Bluetooth
    as WAP bearer, 88-89
    defined, 113
    environments inhabited by, 23-24
    modulation in, 44
    origin of term, 3
    radio used by, 21-24, 24
    topology of, 45-47
Bluetooth Assigned Numbers, 109
Bluetooth devices
    examples of, 20
    OBEX over TCP/IP, 86-87
    OBEX-supporting, 85-86
    operational states of, 57
    power levels of, 25-26
Bluetooth Documents, 137
Bluetooth Host, 114
Bluetooth Service Discovery, 80
Bluetooth Special Interest Group, 135-136
Bluetooth Telephony Control Protocol Specification -Binary (TCS Binary), 87
Bluetooth Test Mode, 94-95
Bluetooth Unit, 114
Bond, 114
Bonding, 114
BT, 114
Byte order, 74

C

CAC, 114
CC, 114
Change link key procedure, 65
Change the current link key procedure, 65
Channel control 55-56
Channel establishment, 115
Channel hopping sequence, 58
Channel Identifier (CID), 73-74
Channels, 73-75, 114
CID (Channel Identifier), 73-74
CL, 115
Clock offset request procedure, 66
CO, 115
CoD, 115
COF, 115
CODEC, 115
Command acceptance, 65
Communications Interfaces
    Interoperability requirements for Bluetooth as a WAP Bearer, 88-89
    IrDA Interoperability, 84-87
    overview, 82
    RFCOMM with TS 07.10, 82-84
    Telephony Control Specification, 87-88
Communications paths complex, 19
Compliance requirements, 95-96
Connect, 115
Connectable device, 115
Connecting, 115
Connection establishment, 115
CONNECTION state, 57
Connections
    defined, 115
    establishing, 69
    sharing, 28
Conscious, 115
Consolidated Glossary, 7, 111

Control of multi-slot packets procedure, 68
Cordless Telephony Profile, 100-101
Core appendices, 107-109
Core document, 4-6
Coverage area, 116
CRC, 116
Creation of a trusted relationship, 116
CTP, 116
CVSD, 116

D

DAC, 116
Data whitening, 53
dB (decibel), 42
dBm, 42
DCE, 116
DCI, 116
De facto Standard, 8
decibel (dB), 42
Detach procedure, 67
Device addressing, 59-60
Device discovery, 116
DH, 117
DIAC, 117
Dial-up Networking Profile, 102-103
Discoverable device, 117
DM, 117
Document structure, 9-12
DT, 117
DTE, 117
DTMF, 117
DUT (Device Under Test), 69, 117
DV, 117

E

Elements, 79
Encryption, 60-61, 108
ENCRYPTION procedure, 65
Error correction, 51-52
Error handling, 70
ETSI, 117

F

Fax Profile, 103
FCC, 117
FEC, 117
FH, 118
FHS, 118
FIFO, 118
File Transfer Profile, 105-106
Flow control, 79
Frequency Hopping Spread Spectrum, 46
FSK, 118
FW, 118

G

GAP, 118
General Response Messages, 65
Generic Access Profile, 99
Generic Object Exchange Profile (GOEP), 104-105
GEOP, 118
GFSK, 118
GIAC, 118
GM, 118
GOEP (Generic Object Exchange Profile), 104-105, 118
GW, 118

H

HA, 118
Hardware implementation, 7
HC, 118
HCI (Host Computer Interface) part of specification
    HCI, 89-90, 118
        HCI Bluetooth Host Controller Interface Functional Specification, 90-92
        HCI RS232 Transport Layer, 92-93
        HCI UART Transport Layer, 93
        HCI USB Transport Layer, 92
    overview, 89-90
Headset application, 32
Headset Profile, 102
HEC, 118
HID, 119
Hold mode procedure, 67
Home PNA, 18
HomePlug Powerline Alliance, 18
Hop selection, 56-58
Host Terminal interface, 119
Hosts, 11
HS, 119
HV, 119
HW, 119

I

IAC, 119
Idle, 119
IEEE, 119
IETF, 119
Industrial Scientific Medical (ISM) band, 38-40
Industry Standard, 8
Initialization, application, 31-32
Inquiry, 119
Inquiry response sequence, 58

Index

Inquiry response substate, 57
Inquiry scan substate, 57
Inquiry sequence, 58
Inquiry substate, 57
Intelligence in devices, 23-24
Interactive conference application, 32
Intercom Profile, 101
Interoperation, 10
Invalid LMP parameters, 70
IP, 119
IPX, 119
IrDA, 120
IrDA interoperability, 85-87
IrMC, 120
IrOBEX (Infrared Object Exchange Protocol), 85-87
ISDN, 120
ISM (Industrial Scientific Medical) band, 38-40, 120
Isochronous user channel, 120
IUT, 120

K

Known, 120
Known device, 120

L

L_CH, 120
L2CA, 120
L2CAP, 121
L2CAP (Logical Link Control and Adaption Protocol) part of specification
    Configuration Message Sequence Charts, 76
    Configuration Parameter Options, 76
    Data Packet Format, 74-75
    General Operation, 73-74
    Implementation Guidelines, 77
    Introduction, 71-73
    overview of section, 70-71

Index

    Signaling, 75
    State Machine, 74
LAN, 121
LAN Access Profile, 103-104
LAP, 121
LAP (lower address part) field, 60
Layers, 9-10
LC (Link Controller), 56-57, 63-64, 121
LCP, 121
LCSS, 121
LFSR, 121
LIAC, 121
Licensing requirements, 95-96
Light medium, 20-21
Link, 121
Link Controller (LC), 56-57, 63-64, 121
Link establishment, 121
Link Manager (LM), 63-64, 121
LM (Link Manager), 63-64, 121
LMP, 121
LMP-authentication, 122
LMP Error Transaction Collision, 70
LMP (Link Manager Protocol) part of specification
    Connection Establishment, 69
    Error Handling, 70
    Format of LMP Messages, 63-64
    General Overview, 63
    introductory notes, 62-63
    PDU summary, 69
    Procedure Rules and Protocol Data Unit Definitions, 64-68
    Test Modes, 69
LMP-pairing, 122
LMP version procedure, 66
LocDev, 122
Logical channels, 52-53, 122
Low power systems, 23
LSB, 122

Index

M

M_ADDR, 122
MAC 1, 122
MAPI, 122
Master response substate, 57
Masters, 15, 45-47, 55-56
ME, 123
Message Sequence Charts (MSCs), 10-12, 109
Microwave radiation levels, 23
MM, 123
MMI, 123
Mode, 123
MS, 123
MSB, 123
MSC, 123
MSCs (Message Sequence Charts), 10-12, 109, 123
MTU, 123
Multicast, 75
MUX, 123

N

NAK, 123
Name discovery, 123
NAME REQUEST procedure, 66
NAP, 123
NAP (non-significant address part) field, 60
new, 123

O

O, 124
OBEX (Object Exchange Protocol), 84-87, 124
Object Push Profile, 104-105
OCF, 124
OGR, 124
OUI (Organizationally Unique Identifier), 59-60

P

Packet, 124
Packet formats, 48-51
PAGE, 124
Page, 124
Page hopping sequence, 56
Page response sequence, 56
PAGE_SCAN, 124
Page scan, 124
Page scan substate, 57
Page substate, 57
Paging, 124
Paging scheme procedure, 68
Paging schemes, 109
Paired device, 125
Pairing procedure, 65
Parts, 9
Path losses, 26-27
PC, 125
PCM, 125
PCMCIA, 125
PDA, 125
PDU, 125
PDUs (Protocol Data Unit), 63-64, 69-70
Physical channel, 125
Physical link, 125
Piconets
    channels in, 55
    defined, 45-46, 73, 126
    hopping sequences, 47
    master/slaves in, 55-56
    slave maximum, 47
    timing, 54
PIM, 126
PIN, 126
PM_ADDR, 126
PnP, 126

Index

POS (Personal Operation Space), 17-18
POTS, 126
Power levels, 25
PPM, 126
PPP, 126
PPP networking, 103
PRBS, 126
Pre-paired device, 126
Private, 126
PRNG, 126
Procedure Rules and Protocol Data Unit definitions, 64-70
Profiles
        Cordless Telephony, 100-101
        defined, 10, 97-99
        Dial-up Networking, 102-103
        Fax, 103
        File Transfer, 105-106
        Generic Access, 99
        Generic Object Exchange, 104
        Headset, 102
        Intercom, 101
        LAN Access, 103-104
        list of defined, 98-99
        Object Push, 104-105
        Serial Port, 101-102
        Service Discovery Profile Application, 100
        Synchronization, 106-107
Profiles document
        defined, 4, 6
        prerequisite for, 8
Programming, 7
Protocol stack, 4-5
Protocols
        communications, 4-5
        defined, 4
PSTN, 126
Public, 127

Index

Q

QoS, 127
Quality of Service (QoS) procedure, 68

R

Radiation levels, 40
Radio medium, 21-22
Radio part of specification
    Frequency Band and Channel Arrangement, 40
    introductory notes, 38-39
    Receiver Characteristics, 41-42
    Scope, 39
    Testing Parameters, 42-43
    Transmitter Characteristics, 41
Radios
    attributes needed, 22, 24
    modulation type used, 39
    receiver characteristics, 41-42
    sensitivity of, 26-27, 41-42
    transmitter characteristics, 41
RAND, 127
Range, 26-27
Reader types, 6-7
Reading order, 8
Reliable, 127
RemDev, 127
Request/response model, 79
RF, 127
RFC, 127
RFCOMM, 127
RFCOMM Client, 127
RFCOMM initiator, 127
RFCOMM part of specification
    Interoperability Requirements for Bluetooth as a WAP Bearer, 88-89
    IrDA interoperability, 84-87
    overview, 82

Index

      Telephony Control Specification, 87
        with TS 07.10, 82-84
RFCOMM Server, 128
RFCOMM Server Channel, 128
RSSI, 128
RX, 128

S

SAP, 128
SAR (Segmentation and Reassembly), 72-73, 128
Scatternet, 128
SCO, 128
SCO (Synchronous Connection-Oriented) links, 48, 128
SCO links procedure, 68
SD, 129
SDDB, 129
SDP, 129
SDP (Service Discovery Protocol) part of specification
      Background Information, 81
      Data Representation, 79
      Example SDP Transactions, 81
      Introduction, 78
      overview, 77-78
      Protocol Description, 79
      Service Attribute Definitions, 79-80
Security, 60-62
Segmentation and Reassembly (SAR), 72-73, 128
Sensitivity, 41-42
SeP, 129
SEQN, 129
Serial port emulation, 83-84
Serial Port Profile, 101-102
Service Discovery, 80, 81, 129
Service Discovery Profile Application Profile, 100
Setup, application, 31
SIG, 129, 135-136
Signaling, 75

Index

Silent device, 130
Slave response substate, 57
Slaves, 15, 45-47, 55-56
Slot offset information procedure, 66
Slots, 40
Sniff mode procedure, 67
Social consequences, 27-29
Sound medium, 20
    See also Audio
Specification parts
    Baseband, 43-62
    HCI (Host Controller Interface), 89-93
    L2CAP (Logical Link Control and Adaption Protocol), 70-77
    LMP (Link Manager Protocol), 62-70
    Radio, 38-43
    RFCOMM, 82-89
    SDP (Service Discovery Protocol), 77-82
SRES, 130
SrvDscApp, 130
SS, 130
SSI, 130
Standard, 8
STANDBY state, 57
Sub-parts, 9
Subscenarios, 11-12
Supported features procedure, 66
SUT, 130
SW, 130
Switch of master-slave role procedure, 66
Synchronization application, 32
Synchronization Profile, 106-107
Synchronous Connection-Oriented (SCO) links, 48, 129

T

TAE, 130
TBD, 130
TC, 130

TCI, 130
TCI (Test Control Interface), 96-97
TCP, 130
TCP/IP, 86-87, 130
TCS, 130
TDD, 130
TDMA (Time Division Multiple Access), 15
Telephony
        Cordless profile, 100-101
        TCS Binary specification, 87-88
Test Control Interface (TCI), 96-97
Testing, 42-43, 87, 94-97
Time Slot, 131
Timing accuracy information request procedure, 66
TL, 131
TLO, 131
TLT, 131
Topology, 45-46
Transmit/Receive Routines, 54
Transmit/Receive Timing, 54
Trusted device, 131
Trusting, 131
TS 07.10 standard, 82-84
TTP, 131
TX, 131

U

UA, 131
UAP, 131
UAP (upper address part) field, 60
UART, 131
UC, 131
UDP, 131
UDP/IP, 131
UI, 132
UIAC, 132
Un-known device, 132

Un-paired device, 132
Unconscious, 132
Unknown, 132
US, 132
USB, 132
UT, 132
UUID, 132

W

Walkie-Talkie Profile, 101
WAP (Wireless Application Protocol), 88-89, 132
Whitening, 53
Wireless media, 20-22
WLANs (Wireless Local Area Networks), 29
WUG, 132